Gambling Online

D & B Publishing

D & B Poker

D & B Bridge

D & B Puzzles

D & B Publishing, PO Box 18, Hassocks, West Sussex BN6 9WR, UK
Tel: 01273 834680, Fax: 01273 831629, e-mail:
info@dandbpublishing.com,
Website: www.dandbpublishing.com

Gambling ONLINE

Angus Dunnington

D&B PUBLISHING
www.dandbpublishing.com

First published in 2004 by D & B Publishing, PO Box 18, Hassocks, West Sussex BN6 9WR

British Library Cataloguing-in-Publication Data
A catalogue record for this book is available from the British Library.

ISBN 1-904468-13-6

All sales enquiries should be directed to:
D & B Publishing, PO Box 18, Hassocks, West Sussex BN6 9WR, UK
Tel: 01273 834680, Fax: 01273 831629, e-mail:
info@dandbpublishing.com,
Website: www.dandbpublishing.com

All screenshots are reproduced by permission and copyright © 2004 the online site from which they are taken.

Cover design by Horatio Monteverde.
Production by Navigator Guides.
Printed and bound in the US by Versa Press.

Contents

Chapter Five: Odds

Chapter Six: Spread Betting

Chapter Seven: The Betting Exchange

Chapter Eight: The Future

Introduction

As far as computers are concerned our views of them tend to differ depending on age. To my father, in his sixties, computers can be intimidating and of no great use. I was born in 1967, so I slot into the generation that first saw the arrival of computers in the family home. They seemed to do very little of any value for something so 'clever' and expensive, other than provide a bit of lunchtime recreation from the boredom of school, a group of boys inviting ourselves around to a friend's house (conveniently located around the corner) to play Space Invaders and Asteroids while eating our sandwiches. When I was about ten or eleven one of my classmates wanted his parents to buy him a computer and, for some reason, his father thought I looked like someone capable of giving sound advice on the subject: 'These computers – what do they compute?'

With a time-machine at my disposal I could have jumped in, whizzed just a couple of decades or so into the future, had a look around and gone straight back with an answer along the lines of: 'Well, at the moment, considering the fact that your son is interested only in games, has absolutely no intention of learning about – nor even the slightest understanding of – how a computer might help him with his education – which, really, it can't, unless of course his future is in learning how to make a computer draw a straight line across the screen – you might as well buy him a skateboard instead' ... and then I could have added 'But when your grandchildren are my age technology will have moved on beyond your wildest dreams. They will be able to use a computer to access just about all the knowledge mankind has accumulated throughout history by pressing a couple of keys, learn languages, watch a live broadcast of people looking around the shop windows in New York, send messages to their friends across the world – who will be able to reply within seconds. This is because worldwide networks will connect all the millions and millions of computers... Meanwhile your son – who lost all his lunch money for the week playing cards round at Keith's house – will have moved with the times, embracing these fantastic technological advances with a gusto you wouldn't expect to see in him now because he gives the impression that he's not the sharpest tool in the box. Oh yes – apart from being able not only to switch a computer on but turn it off as well, he'll devote hours of his spare time to sitting in front of his investment (they're not cheap, but everybody seems to have one – even in Belgium), exploiting the great potential of this super 'inter-network' to look at lots and lots of photographs of rude women, play poker for real money in a special 'virtual' casino, chasing cards and losing his lunch money for work – usually to people who live in the same tiny village – population: 12 – in northern Sweden... Yeah, things will be a lot different soon enough, you'll see...' ('Oh, good. Sounds nice. What was that bit about rude women again?)

Today, of course, the mystery has gone. Ask a ten year-old what can be done with a computer and you'll need a good hour or so to take in his reply. Chances are the youngster will already be aware that people gamble online. Even my dad's generation seem to finally appreciate what's on offer. In fact when the ostensibly anti-gambling Dunnington senior is not scouring the internet for victims on a betting exchange or studying the finance markets he's been known to win the occasional $20 entry fee, 18-player 'Sit n' Go' poker tournaments on **Pokerstars.com**.

The internet – everybody seems to be doing it. And if everybody is doing it, then it is not surprising to see those in the know falling over themselves to provide us with the facility, while we're 'tuned in', to partake in the second oldest pastime in history – gambling.

Angus Dunnington,

November 2004

Chapter One

Online Gambling Revolution

Hard Work has a Future Payoff – Laziness Pays off Now

I don't remember where I came across this cynical yet admirable observation on life but I guess it could have been in a men's magazine. While I don't condone laziness, it is nevertheless a characteristic quite common amongst gamblers, of whom many – myself included – were originally attracted to the world of gambling by the promise of financial gain for (ideally) an absolute minimum of effort. And why not? The fact that we all know this to be quite untrue is of no relevance because the potential returns compared with spending time on something 'constructive' is worth the slight adjustment of a few real world boundaries. The genuine lazy gambler, of course, has hitherto been obliged to engage in the physical inconvenience of actually making the journey to the casino...

The Changing face of the Gambler

As a boy, when I first began to understand what a high street bookmaker was, it seemed that the typical client was male, aged around fifty, working class, smoker, an avid reader of a tabloid newspaper, in the most part a follower of horse racing and – significantly – almost resigned to handing over his cash to the people behind the counter (with whom he would always be on first name terms), yet not expecting to be given much in return.

When I started going to casinos in the UK I noticed that the people were quite different, apparently self-appointed gambling crusaders on a mission to beat the 'house' with systems, guile, guts or – if all these failed – snazzy clothes. The friendly banter 'enjoyed' in the bookmaker when nobody's horse came in was a far cry from the condescending looks and sarcastic comments witnessed at the blackjack tables when you were held responsible for your fellow players losing because you asked for another card (or opted against taking another – it doesn't matter, you're still to blame).

Travelling far and wide as a full-time chess player took me to casinos all over the world, from the south of France, for example, where everything is aimed at providing the customer with a luxurious environment in which to part with his money, to Nigeria where, depending on the casino, only the latter part of the relationship matters (even if this means responding to 'stand', 'no card' or 'this time absolutely NO card!' when the player has, let's say, 19, by happily flipping across another...).

Generally, the common denominator in these often rather cosmopolitan casinos was a shared enjoyment for thirty/forty-somethings (or older), an entertaining evening out. My recollections of all these experiences might not be completely accurate, of course, and a 'good' time is the last thing on a serious gambler's mind, the mercenary player thinking only in terms of leaving with more money than he walked in with. But, essentially, only gambling converts have tended to regularly frequent gambling establishments.

Online Casinos

So now that the casino and the bookmaker – manifesting themselves in the albeit two-dimensional form provided by the computer screen – are available in the home, what are we to make of them? And what kind of people gamble online?

Perhaps I've spent too much time immersing myself in online gambling this year, but it appears that whatever the subject matter of a web page these days, we're never far from an ad for an online casino, tempting us with the ubiquitous bonus and dozens of razzmatazzy ways of giving them our cash.

Assuming we have a decent idea of what traditional casinos and book-makers are, what are we to expect from their online equivalents? Initially the whole experience can be rather intimidating (particularly if you are not too well acquainted with the internet), not least finding something suitable and, subsequently, making the decision to actually join. The selection can be daunting because, even during the last couple of years, the industry has exploded. In fact when the idea for this book first came about my intention was to sift through and review a number of sites but, with the terrain altering so rapidly – resulting, I believe, in a more level and bountiful playing field – this is no longer necessary. A simple search on Google will point us in the right direction, we just need to know what to do when we get there.

Like a busy restaurant's continued custom serving as a good advert for what is on offer, the global clients of online gambling are gathering at such a pace, and bringing their money along, that we shouldn't be too apprehensive about testing out the water. Internet sports betting, for instance, has overtaken even Las Vegas-based sports books, a 2002 US Congressional Report putting worldwide online gambling revenues at over $4 billion (roughly half of this from US residents) compared with less than $2 billion in 2002 in (legal) Nevada. Moreover, had credit card companies not obstructed transfers to offshore casinos and gambling companies the global online market would have reached $5 billion.

The Online Gambling Family

As the internet gambling family grows it is only natural that revenue will continue to increase, and the easy availability (more choice, better prices, better deals etc.) afforded us by the internet might well lead to traditional bricks & mortar firms taking stock of the situation and coming up with new ideas. 'If you can't beat them, join them' might be an idea, but this is often neither practical nor legal – a matter we will come to later. In the meantime, we are being drawn at an alarming rate to online operators.

A nationwide U.S. survey carried out by OpinionPlace (Digital Marketing Services) for America Online (from mid December 2003 to mid January 2004) revealed some interesting facts about gaming (not necessarily gambling) online. Men are more likely than women to play online for money but, while men spent more time on the Internet than women (23.2 hours per week compared with 21.6 hours), for women over 40, some 9.1 of these hours involved online gaming, whereas for men this was only 6.1 hours of the total online time. With gambling in general becoming more mainstream, the notion that women who enjoy the relaxation and social interaction that the internet provides might well lead to them joining the ranks of internet gamblers promises to further swell the ranks of online gambling. At the time of writing, for example, the internet poker explosion is fast attracting women.

A report in the Guardian newspaper (UK) said that, according to media consultancy firm Screen Digest, the so-called 'bored housewife' is turning to online gambling. Internet tracking agency Nielsen found that 64 per cent of online punters were women, and 60 per cent of these were married. The conclusion was that an increase in the number of people with internet access combined with an increasingly elderly population with sufficient free time had helped generate a huge demand for online gaming, with gambling becoming more popular. In fact among the main online gambling attractions were bingo, casino games such as slots and roulette, and poker.

Ladbrokes, for example, noted that on their sites women are coming to online gambling at a phenomenal rate. About 16 per cent of women had tried poker in some form or other and, although this is still only around a third of the men's figure, by the time you're reading this I would expect the male-female gap to have narrowed considerably.

Additionally, adults are not only more likely than teenagers to play online games daily, but also more likely to do so through the night. But don't be fooled by the adults' apparent monopoly here. Colleges, for example, are populated exclusively by the internet generation, the recent sudden interest in poker sure to spill out into other areas of internet gambling.

Incidentally, for those of you living in Washington, D.C. who are prone to spending considerably long periods doing nothing but gambling online – you are by no means alone. For some reason Washington residents are among the highest to prepare for a trip to Las Vegas or other casino cities by 'practising' online, not surprisingly registering a nationally high level of missed appointments such as dates or job interviews due to being too busy gambling online. Obviously this should not be condoned and, as in life, moderation is the key.

Another example of the growth of online gaming comes from the perhaps unlikely source of Belgium. When I lived there as a professional chess player in the early 1990s a few casinos offered the usual games and slots and so on. But now the facility to gamble online has taken hold, with a recent government report putting the number of Belgians actively gambling on the internet in 2003 at 150,000, spending somewhere in the region of 27 million euros (almost US$32.5 million at the time of writing). These figures are expected to rise considerably this year, prompting a special Gaming Commission to take a look. More than a thousand gamblers have banned themselves – with the help, in fact, of the Gaming Commission – from entering B&M casinos, but it is feared that the ease with which individuals can gamble online could be a problem.

What these findings do demonstrate is the extent of the convenience we are afforded by the internet. Convenience is paramount these days, and the facility to gamble – be it for pennies or much more – without having to leave your chair (never mind walking out the door), more or less whenever you choose and in the privacy of your own home makes for an attractive prospect in an age when we have become used to home comforts and technology.

It doesn't matter any more if we've never stepped foot in a casino, filled in a betting slip or had anything to do with any kind of traditional gambling. Thanks to the internet the now vast world of gambling can come straight to us. It's no longer necessary to be part of a special group of people who only used to come out at night – now we're all special. There is no typical player. We are all typical players.

Gambling at Work

Not only is there a growing band of people who have either switched from bricks and mortar casinos to the online versions or simply begun their gambling experience online at home, but the attraction of the internet as a medium for gambling has seen a spilling over into life at work.

In April 2004 a survey carried out by US firms Cerberian, a provider of internet content filtering solutions, and SonicWALL, internet security specialists, produced some interesting facts about the internet 'habits' of office workers, of whom 2400 were canvassed. Perhaps not surprisingly, a number of office workers are – rather than bringing their work home with them – in fact taking their penchant for online gambling to work. The report found that 32 percent of people have seen co-workers surf gambling sites, while as much as 85 percent have seen co-workers surfing sports-related websites, these usually linking to sports wagering sites. While I obviously don't support such goings on, it is nevertheless another sign of the times as far as online gambling is concerned.

How does it Work?

Online gambling software falls into two categories – download and no-download. For the sakes of flexibility and choice casinos would do well to provide both options. No-download casino software using Java, Flash or Shockwave technology is played within a web browser and uses software that is already installed on the player's computer, the files being sufficiently small to enable them to be transferred for each playing session. In the early days no-download software was considered the lesser of the two options due to its poorer graphics, but the quality has since improved. Consequently those casinos that feature the no-download facility tend to be successful in attracting new player signups, potential customers being under no obligation to commit time and their computer's resources in order to test out games. Nevertheless, no-download games can fall foul of glitches in a player's pre-installed software.

With downloadable software an application is loaded and saved on to the player's computer; this takes up resources but affords the player the advantage of immediate play, which is why this is the more popular option with those who intend to play on a more regular basis.

To conclude, no-download casino software does a good job in attracting browsers – often through play-for-free facilities – and subsequently turning them into buyers, whereas download software has a reputation for being of slightly better quality and of more long-term convenience.

Choosing an Online Casino

Before joining it is worth, in the case of a casino, for example, having a tour around the site, taking advantage of the facility many casinos offer (and so they should) that allows you to play for fun.

Give the following points some consideration:

Graphics, Speed, Sound etc.

Is the overall playing experience to your liking? There seems little point joining if something about the presentation of the games you intend playing is not right. You will always be able to find a site that suits your personal requirements.

Software

See what kind of software is used, perhaps visiting the website of the software producer itself (see below).

Customer Support

Have a go at contacting Customer Support, and see in what form(s) this is available – live chat (very useful when you get a response), telephone (toll-free), email etc.

Dig

In order to feel as secure as is realistically possible you might spend some time checking out the financial stability of the casino, whether it has insurance, licensing and so on. Click on the About Us tab. Does the casino have any (independently judged) awards and affiliation to respected 'watchdog' bodies such as the Interactive Gaming Council or eCogra (see below).

Rules

Get acquainted with the rules, just in case. If you have a problem – particularly with your cash in the casino's accounts! – you don't want to fall foul of some obscure piece of small print.

Consult other Players

Word of mouth is always useful – better to learn of good (or bad) experiences of customers than to blindly follow the casino's own self-recommendation. The best way to do this is to visit forums, where advice is always available.

Privacy

Make sure your details are safe with the casino, that their policy ensures that these will not be passed on elsewhere.

Obviously some factors are more important than others, depending on how you see the whole business of the internet. It is worth seeing how experienced online gamblers approach the selection issue. In December 2003 Harrods Casino (**www.harrods-casino.com**) released the findings of in-depth telephone research that asked experienced gamblers their selection criteria for playing online casinos.

Here are the results in descending order of importance:

1. Confidence and trust in the casino, especially the importance of brands with which they have previously interacted. Players emphasized their concern over gambling at unknown brands as they could not be confident they would be offered a fair game or even be paid their winnings.

2. Quick and efficient cash-outs.

3. Favourable odds of winning.

4. Responsive and individualised customer service.

5. Ease, speed and quality of play.

6. Sign-up and other bonuses.

Note the long-term priorities here, with the emphasis firmly on confidence in the site itself, familiarity being particularly important. Of course this is no different to gambling life in general – I am not going to hand over my hard earned cash to an unknown back street bookmakers when there's a Ladbrokes around the corner, and nor would I accept better than evens odds on Black on Mr Big's home made roulette table. Bonuses are obviously an attraction of sorts, but we shouldn't allow their lure to cloud our judgement at the cost of good old-fashioned trust. The very brand name of Harrods, for example, is so well known and respected throughout the world that whatever venture it undertakes is guaranteed to receive respect, thus affording it a head start on an identical project introduced by myself, for instance... Incidentally this research also found that Blackjack was the favourite game of the respondents, followed by roulette, slots and baccarat.

Other research has found that as much as 20 percent of website visitors will soon abandon sites that they don't consider to be user-friendly. Put in the simple, fundamental and crucial context of clients' money, this demonstrates the importance for sites – regardless of whether they offer sports betting, traditional casino games or other forms of gambling – to provide their customers with a comfortable, helpful and easy to understand online environment. If the general look and feel of a site is not properly addressed by those who run it, then potential customers might not take the plunge and deposit their cash, while existing clients can nowadays be so easily enticed elsewhere. This is why we are suitably impressed by those sites that seek to constantly maintain a certain level of user-oriented facilities and features, with regular improvements and updates serving to hold on to our patronage.

Licensed to Thrill

Given the profits of online casinos and gambling firms, as well as the pace with which operators can become major players within the industry, it is not surprising that new sites are constantly emerging on the scene. But how are they licensed? And where? You would be surprised, for not only does online gambling serve to demonstrate just how easy it is to lose a few dollars in such a short time (almost without us noticing, in fact...), but seeing the various places around the world in which these firms are officially based is quite a good lesson in geography.

Don't be fooled into believing that online casinos with, for example, Monte Carlo or Mississippi as part of their name are actually operating within a dice throw of the Cote D'Azur or the great gambling river. The snappy or stylish sounding site names are simply the first step in painting a suitably attractive, alluring picture with which prospective customers feel comfortable. Qualifying for and securing a license requires those behind these firms to venture further a field in the search of a recognised, legal jurisdiction from where to operate, and for internet entrepreneurs in some countries this isn't always convenient.

When the pioneers were taking the first steps into online gambling the jurisdictions situated mainly around the Caribbean, in Antigua, Costa Rica, Dominica and (later) Curacao. As the industry's potential was becoming more apparent other, more industrially developed countries got involved, with Australia throwing its hat in the jurisdiction ring. This was followed by the Mohawk Territory of Kahnawake in Canada, which was the first North American jurisdiction to introduce licenses for online gambling.

Then came Europe in the shape of Gibraltar, the Isle of Man and Alderney providing the whole internet gambling with the 'respectability' afforded the industry by the facility to be licensed from a U.K. jurisdiction.

As I have mentioned elsewhere in this book, with countries responding to the growth of internet gambling among their own nationals by investigating the pros and cons of offering licenses from their shores, and with England taking a lead in terms of a realistic approach to gambling in general, it is surely only a matter of time until certain other countries more positively explore the implications of allowing what are essentially domestic enterprises to finally operate within domestic jurisdictions.

In the meantime, regardless of the fact that countries which are neither very well known or, indeed, very wealthy are hosting what have become big businesses, a would-be operator must demonstrate certain qualifications in order to be secure the necessary regulation (moreover the jurisdictions require a respected, confidence inspiring environment in which to maintain any successful level of competition with their growing number of rivals). Therefore, as would be the case for anyone planning to set up a bricks and mortar casino in Las Vegas, for example, the online casino applicant must demonstrate a sufficient level of competency (and respectability) and so on even to be part of the process. Fundamental factors such as having the financial ability to actually operate an online casino and manage the payouts is obviously imperative.

Typically, having met all the conditions, the applicant's software then comes under scrutiny (security, fair games, payouts, ability to cope with heavy traffic and peak periods of activity, general reliability etc.).

As for the cost to the prospective operator, depending on the quality and range of facilities offered by a particular jurisdiction, annual licensing fees can be anything from a round, tidy sum of $50,000 (in itself no small potatoes) to a staggering $1 million...

As well as licensing fees and local taxes, the operator must also be prepared to provide the host authorities with accounts and relevant reports, and constantly be able to demonstrate that the initial requirements are being maintained.

Safety & Standards

A website might look great, sound great, claim to be great and be recommended by enthusiastic but commission-based sites awash with banner ads and inviting links, but we would prefer to be guided by more independent opinion. Obviously there are numerous factors to be taken into consideration before parting with our cash, certain pros and cons can be interpreted in different ways and, as we have seen, one potential customer's criteria might well be quite unlike another's. Moreover, other than the fairly fundamental things to look out for there are some key issues and features regarding online gambling sites that we either undervalue or even fail to appreciate but that experts in various aspects of the industry believe to be of considerable importance. With this in mind it is reassuring that the explosion of internet gambling and the accompanying flood of sites we are now exposed to has prompted the setting up of organisations aimed at placing a growing number of the would-be bigger online gambling operators under the microscope.

One such body that is a welcome arrival to the vast world of online gambling is eCOGRA, the acronym standing for eCommerce and Online Gaming Regulation and Assurance. This is an independent, non-profit organisation designed specifically to protect us internet players by imposing strict operating rules – known as eGAP or eCOGRA Generally Accepted Practices – on its members.

We should remember that with sites based in numerous countries that have quite diverse laws and regulations, it is (thus far) impossible to actually police internet gambling firms worldwide, but this does not preclude the possibility that these companies can voluntarily abide by the strict player-friendly 'rules' of a well respected regulatory body that, to some extent, assumes a policing role.

Just as it is imperative for reputable businesses such as travel agents or global superstores to sign up to the rules of relevant standards commissions and so on (thereby committing themselves to specific requirements and trading methods), it is equally important for those who run internet gambling sites with a view to carving out a healthy share of the market and establishing a solid, long-term client base to be associated with an organisation such as eCOGRA.

Displaying a willingness to adhere to certain requirements and methods of conducting business as well as being prepared to have the site come under the scrutiny of a team of independent inspectors induces confidence in clients. Satisfied players can lead only to better business, so eCOGRA is a win-win situation for both players and the casinos that meet the organisation's requirements to a level that justifies the eCOGRA Seal. Having seen so many gushing 'in-house' awards plastered over so many gambling sites it is easy to be suspicious of a site being afforded an official seal of integrity and standard but, in this case at least, the requirements for approval are detailed and strict and devised with the player in mind.

Applicants are required to implement a detailed list of eGAP requirements covering every player-sensitive area of operations. This includes informed and contactable Support, tough Accounting and financial requirements to ensure fast payouts, dispute resolution systems and a host of other services regarded as necessary for a casino to operate effectively. When the applicant is confident that eGAP is in place inspection teams consisting of qualified and independent professionals are brought in for verification (or to point out necessary actions) using the proprietary outcomes testing procedure developed by PricewaterhouseCoopers, a large, internationally respected professional services group. Known as the Total Gaming Transaction Review, the system uses sophisticated analysis techniques to review every single gaming transaction at casinos bearing the eCOGRA Seal. Anomalies will automatically trigger further examination.

Those casinos that pass the inspection are awarded the Seal and are required to display this prominently on-site, the process continuing with a variety of ongoing methods being used by the organisation to monitor operations. Additionally, applicant casinos must use software from providers that have themselves been rigorously tested for probity, games fairness and solid backend capability by eCOGRA contracted teams. The London staff includes a Fair Gaming Advocate to whom complaints can be made online in the event that any player-casino dispute cannot be resolved.

At the time of writing inspections carried out on leading casinos during 2003/2004 have resulted in over 40 operations meeting the requirements, and with integrity such a key issue these days, expect the eCOGRA umbrella to grow.

eCOGRA Seal Practices and Associated Objectives

The integrity of the eCOGRA seal is principally dependent on the following process:

- Whether the seal requirements are sufficient and appropriate.
- The extent to which operators and software providers adhere to these requirements.
- The effectiveness of the procedures adopted by the Audit Panel firms to ensure compliance with these requirements.

An exhaustive and detailed schedule of requirements encompassing all areas of online gaming relating to fair gaming practices are incorporated into eGAP. Here is a summary of each practice and its related objective, which really does bring home to us, the customer, what is involved for those who set up and successfully maintain internet casinos.

Player Protection

1 Payment to and Receipts from Players
Payment requests/receipts shall be efficiently and promptly attended to and payments/receipts shall be completely and accurately processed.

2 Minimum Information Requirements
Seal holders shall be required to adequately record certain minimum information relating to player and game activity.

3 Minimum Security Requirements
Information security policies and procedures shall be implemented and maintained to ensure the availability, integrity and confidentiality of gaming operations.

4 Responsible Gaming

A responsible gaming environment that actively discourages problematic gambling shall be established, enforced and monitored.

5 Player and Game Funds

Player balances and game funds shall be sufficiently covered by on demand funds.

6 Player Information

Player accounts shall be managed and accounted for in a secure, safe and efficient environment. The privacy and confidentiality of all player information submitted at any point in time shall be protected from unauthorised disclosure.

Fair Gaming

7 Software Development and Maintenance

Software shall be developed, implemented and maintained in a manner representative of best practice standards.

8 Total Gaming Transaction Review

Games shall be random, independent and fair.

9 Server Connectivity Requirements

Minimum game server connectivity requirements shall be met to ensure that players are protected from losses due to connectivity problems.

10 General Game Characteristics

Seal holders shall adhere to game characteristics that ensure a fair game for a player.

11 Disaster Recovery

eCOGRA seal holders shall be able to demonstrate that they can recover from a system disaster.

12 System Malfunctions

Both the player and eCOGRA's seal holders shall be protected from system and hardware malfunctions.

Responsible Conduct

13 Anti-Money Laundering

Preventative and detective controls addressing money-laundering and fraud risks shall be documented and implemented according to the relevant points in the Financial Action Task Force (FATF) guidelines.

14 Responsible Advertising and Promotions

The seal holder will ensure that players are not misled through advertising or promotional activities, and will ensure that the terms and conditions of their promotions are followed.

15 Probity Checks

All key individuals and entities involved with members and operators should be credible and not have criminal records.

The Review of System Software

As for the gaming software, this is clearly one of the key areas that must be addressed by a body such as eCOGRA, which has developed a highly comprehensive and practical system testing methodology called Total Gaming Transaction Review (TGTR), an 'outcome-based verification' approach that deviates substantially from the commonly adopted testing of source code which has traditionally been used in the land-based gaming environment (and which has been commonly adopted in the online environment). This process may be undertaken with minimal disruption to the software provider and operator business activities (which is good for the player), and involves a thorough analysis of every transaction for every game by an independent and trusted third party.

It is important to note that the involvement of more than one independent party in investigating and subsequently monitoring internet casinos and other gambling operators is that each has its own obligation to fulfil and reputation to maintain, meaning that those internet firms coming on board must perform at the required level in order to achieve all-round success and to continue the integrity of those involved.

Hopefully the proliferation of online gambling ventures will prompt yet more support for organisations like eCOGRA, allowing would-be internet gamblers to dip their toes into the ocean that is online gaming with maximum confidence.

You can read more about eCOGRA on its website at www.ecogra.org

Software

In the early days of internet gambling forums and chatrooms would feature discussions about what was on offer at this or that particular website. Not only do the modern, experienced online gambling enthusiasts now have favourite websites and games, but they also become attached to specific software features. These preferences could be based on the actual mechanics of how a game is played out, useful extras and tools, the software's general feel, look, sound and other cosmetic features. Consequently the software providers are constantly seeking to both maintain a competitive standard and introduce their own special flavour and characteristics in order to keep up with the pack, with new players coming on the scene as the industry continues to expand.

Players are becoming increasingly aware of what is on offer and which sites feature whose software, so with this in mind, here is a brief run-down of software providers that you might be interested in checking out. Some might currently supply only one or two sites, but that is not to say further expansion will not see them competing with the better known, bigger hitters in the future, so each firm is worth tapping into a web search when you have the time.

Top Ten Software Providers

At the time of writing the software providers whose offerings can be seen on the most sites are listed below (followed by the number of sites):

World Gaming	133
Microgaming	100
RealTime Gaming	65
iGlobal Media	59
Interactive Gaming Systems	51
Playtech	50
dot com Entertainment Group	48
Aqua Online	45
Boss Media	44
IQ-Ludorum	44

Others

AcTax Infotech, ADLM Gaming, American TAB Limited, ASF Software Inc, Atlantic West Gaming, Avesta Design Studio, B3W Group, Betting-Corp, BIANOR, Bingonet, BingoWorkz, Byworth Investments, Casino Village on Net, Casinova Software Ltd, Chartwell Technology, ClickEffect Inc, Clock Media, Columbia Exchange Systems, CryptoLogic, Cyber-Bookies, Diamond Digital Systems, Digital Gaming Solutions Inc, eBet Online, EGET, Electronic Technology Solutions, Exciting Games, Finsoft Limited, FutureBet Systems, GamblingSoftware.com, GameLogic, Gaming Logix, GFed Software, GGBet Limited, GlobalCom Inc, GlobalDip Gaming, Glory Worldwide Holdings, Grand Virtual, Greatbet, Hayes Media, i2Corp.com, iChance, IGW Software, iNet Software, INNOCO, Internet Bingo Ventures, ITOS, Kismet Studios, Las Vegas From Home Entertainment, Leap Frog Gaming, LegalPlay Entertainment, Lodel Enterprises, Max Skyweb Corporation, Mercedes Software, Micropower, My-Casino-Builder.Com, Net Entertainment, Netserve, Nova Internet, OddsON, Ongame, Online Gaming Systems, Online Innovations, Orbis Technology (OpenBet), OutBound Systems, Oyster Commerce, Parspro,

PDMS – Professional Data Management Services, PokerBlaster, Pro Wager Systems, Progressive Gaming Software, QuadCard Entertainment, Random Logic RightNow, Sportsbook Solutions, Inc, Star Media, Tain AB, Unified Gaming Software, Valora Software, Wager21, WagerLogic, WagerWorks, Windows Casino, Wirex S.r.l., Zabadoo.

Chapter Two

Show Them Your Money

After joining an online gambling operator we can't take our first step on the road to riches until we have first deposited money into our account. My mother isn't the only computer owner with an aversion to making financial transactions over the internet, but anything involving money – both on and off line – requires a certain level of caution and aforethought. Fortunately, we are at no more risk when moving money in and out of online casinos, sportsbooks and poker rooms and so on than we are when dealing in any other such transaction over the internet.

With the online gambling industry now such big business, each firm that endeavours to hold onto a profitable share of the market is doing its utmost to maintain the highest standards, which obviously include the safe and secure payments from and to its customers.

Typically, casinos use 128-bit encryption security to protect all transfers of information and funds, this confidentiality and security being just as safe as when we execute similar online transactions with banks and other financial institutions. Remember that customer details should be stored on a secure server protected by the latest firewall systems, while the casinos should also not be in the habit of passing on members' personal details to a third party. Look out for precise details of such assurances as soon as you're ready to sign up, and when depositing money check the padlock symbol that confirms the site is indeed secure.

Depositing Options

Fortunately there are several ways to make deposits, the most convenient being with a credit or debit card. When this is an option it is of course very convenient but, recently, obstacles have been put in the way of some players because banks and credit card companies have made policy changes. For example at the beginning of 2004 VISA stopped accepting withdrawals from online casinos back on to customers' credit cards. Of course for those affected this can be an inconvenience (winnings can be paid via a banker's draft) and, while for other players moving money in and out of casinos with a card is still the chosen mode of transfer, these changes have led to other forms of transaction growing in popularity.

Here is a list of options that should prove useful in helping you get started. Some casinos that find certain payment methods more convenient than others might even offer a bonus to customers using particular options, while complete customer privacy is common among these payment companies, thus affording players anonymity when dealing with online casinos.

NETELLER

Canadian company NETELLER, which had its shares listed in April 2004 on the Alternative Investment Market (AIM) of the London Stock Exchange, provides an excellent, free online money transfer service – effectively acting as an online wallet. Consequently, funds can be accessed and transferred at any time.

After opening a NETELLER account customers can deposit, withdraw, and transfer funds with a host of internet companies, with online casino transactions a speciality. Various forms of transaction are available, and credit card information is kept private from the merchants thanks to NETELLER being the central body to and from which each payment is made. Visit **www.neteller.com** for more information and to open an account.

FirePay

A FirePay Personal Account is a (free) web-based bank account that works along the lines of a debit card, the money deposited into the account being used to pay for goods and services online. Again there is the convenience of being able to move money backwards and forwards around online casinos. Visit **www.firepay.com** to register.

Citadel

Provided by Citadel Commerce, this is an electronic internet check product which has allowed those without credit cards (or those who have reached their limit) to perform online transactions. A good feature of this service is that authentication is done immediately (online). Please note that thus far customers must have a US dollar checking account in the United States while Canadians must also have a Canadian dollar account. Visit **www.citadelcommerce.com** for more information.

900pay

900pay provides a convenient online purchasing method that charges the deposit to the customer's telephone bill so that no credit card or bank account is required. From what I gather it is necessary to ensure there is no 900-service block on the telephone line in order to use 900pay, but I suggest visiting **www.900pay.com** for details.

TeleBuy

TeleBuy is another telephone-based deposit method, using an e-check payment system that requires only bank account information and a telephone. However, here the charges don't appear on the telephone bill as the telephone is used only to confirm the transaction, which can take between 2-4 business days (funds must clear).

N.B. Both TeleBuy and 900pay are currently available only to US residents with US dollar bank accounts in the United States.

Central Coin

One of the more recent additions for online gamblers – and therefore (at least at the time of writing) available with fewer operators than the more established firms – Central Coin is another central medium to and from which payments can be made. After depositing funds into a Central Coin account using a credit card or an e-check the now familiar process is simple and safe, again with the customer's personal information kept confidential. Visit **www.centralcoin.com** for more information.

Prepaid ATM

PrePaidATM is effectively an ATM card that is not tied to a bank account. It can be used with online firms where debit cards are accepted, there are several options for depositing and funds can be received at thousands of ATM machines worldwide. For US customers the good news is that money can be sent anywhere within the United States in a matter if seconds, while there is no need for personal details to be revealed with each transaction. Apparently there is small fee for payment processing. Visit **www.prepaidatm.com** for details.

Click2Pay

Similar to NETELLER, Click2Pay is a fast, secure internet wallet that is chiefly used by US and UK customers, with the dollar, UK pound and Euro currencies in accepted usage.

EcoCard

Another payment system to benefit Europeans, this method is particularly useful for those who don't qualify for a credit card. Using a chain of EcoCard affiliated banks, EcoCard is part of a modern funding system that allows European players to carry out transactions in their own country and using local currency. Customers are also guaranteed confidentiality regarding personal details. Visit **www.ecocard.com** for details.

Moneybookers

Moneybookers provides a system in which money can be sent from a credit card and transferred to and from a bank account via email. FSA regulated and supporting over 20 currencies, this is a convenient service for Europeans. Visit **www.moneybookers.com** for details.

Wire Transfers & Money Orders

Simply sending funds from a bank account to a casino by the tried and trusted wire transfer might not be in the spirit of the internet era but is nevertheless a safe and secure way of dealing with online casinos, who are themselves happy with this foolproof payment method. Meanwhile, if none of the above methods is suitable, then there is the money order option.

Now that we have made a couple of people happy – namely the casino manager and accountant – by safely depositing *our* money into the casino's account, it is time to reflect upon what we intend to do with it. Of course we should have thought about this already, but we were too excited about getting started...

Here are some general thoughts over which to ponder while you adjust your computer chair to ultra-laid back mode, in readiness for the hours of online gambling fun to come:

Bankroll

Set – and stick to – a specific budget. This applies to both long and short-term planning and must be taken seriously right from the beginning, although it is surprising just how casual we can become when it comes to keeping track of the finances. In fact I would be prepared to wager that most of you will have read that line and sensibly and wholeheartedly agreed with it, only to ignore the advice should *that* moment of emptiness (your account, that is) arrive.

While most players hope for some kind of success through gambling on the web, in the main it should not come as a great shock to lose money, so it is essential to be both prepared for this eventuality and to subsequently take any reverses in your stride. Rejoicing and adopting an all-conquering attitude after a nice win while burying your head in the sand when things aren't going your way is a recipe for disaster, so remember to be constantly conscious of your finances, regardless of results.

Don't Lose Your Shirt

Hopefully this is ridiculously obvious advice but (just in case) NEVER play with money you can't avoid to lose! Similarly it is foolish to decide on a realistic bankroll and a period of time during which you intend to play if you then select games and tables that require minimum units and betting levels beyond your outlay.

Don't Chase Your Losses

The best method of avoiding the common bad habit of reacting to losses by bringing more money to the table is to decide upon a set amount of money for a playing session and quit if and when it's gone, regardless of how quickly this unfortunate point might arise. It can be frustrating to sit down after a day at work with the intention of risking, say $100 at everyonesawinner.com, only to see the money disappear after a few minutes, but it is worth getting used to quitting immediately. Otherwise there is a danger of drifting into a potentially hazardous chasing mentality which, ultimately, is neither enjoyable nor good money management. Losing is part of the game and is sure to happen over two, three, four and more consecutive playing sessions every now and then, so there's no point stretching or breaking what should be sensible, long-term rules just to try and even the score.

Don't Chase Your Wins

Just as we should be in no hurry to redress the balance after suffering a reverse, nor should winning prompt us to suddenly step up a gear and increase the stake for no other reason than to win more money. Remember that budget considerations should be a factor in determining if and by how much bets might be increased.

Don't Blow Your Winnings

Given that we can expect losing sessions to crop up more than we'd like, then decent wins should be looked at realistically, from a 'real life' point of view. Starting out with a specific bankroll – let's say $500 – that we are prepared to lose in its entirety does not mean that any sizeable winnings automatically have to stay put. When, for example, $500 quickly becomes $1000 after a fortuitous period (or, if we prefer, due to admirable displays of skill), there are three courses of action to consider. Some players simply see their bankroll as having expanded yet retaining the same initial value and are therefore happy to continue as per normal. They were prepared to part with $500 when they first embarked on the journey into online gambling and nothing has changed, other than finding themselves being able to keep the fire burning.

New players in particular run the risk of interpreting initially positive results as an indication that a pattern has been set and more is to follow. This is a worrying example of potentially dangerous overconfidence that can prompt the ambitious – some would say, naive – player to 'up the ante' and even harbour the notion that winnings will increase by adding yet more money to the cause, the usual result being the eventual overall loss of more than the original $500.

Live a Little

I would recommend the non-gambling option when considerable winnings lead to a bigger bankroll of simply skimming off part of the profit for use in the real world, leaving roughly the original amount in play. This might seem quite a boring, matter-of-fact and even timid thing to do compared with the more macho let-it-ride approach – which is why so many of us (I include myself here) will nevertheless manage to talk ourselves out of actually putting the money to good use. But while gambling is popular for all kinds of reasons, we can be forgiven for believing that the ultimate aim is to emerge from all the excitement with more money than when we started, and it is a nice feeling to be able to gamble with 'free' money or, put into the gambler's 'them and us' context, the casino's money. Moreover, it is most definitely not a nice feeling to contemplate what should be done with money won, deciding against keeping it and then lose the same amount (and more) soon after. By getting into the habit of occasionally moving money from the casino to the bank, rather than the (usual) other way around, we at least appreciate the fact that these cyberchips and credits we are playing with or paying out in order to gamble do actually have genuine value, while tasting the profits also reminds us of what is a fundamental aim in gambling – winning the casino's money.

However, newcomers to internet gambling should, before cashing out early in the campaign, consider the possibility that any gains can quite easily be followed by (even greater) losses. Fluctuations – of which the extremes can indeed be extreme, depending on the type of game being played and betting patterns used – are certainly to be expected, so cashing out too much might mean subsequently having to replenish the bankroll should results start to take the negative route.

The Dangers of Anonymity

Ironically, the greatest attraction of online gambling – namely that we can spend as much time as we please wagering our money while enjoying all the creature comforts of home – also introduces a serious and potentially destructive issue connected with the very anonymity we desired in the first place when opting to live the casino and betting experience on our own terms (rather than those thrust upon us by B&M casinos).

Unfortunately for many online gamblers, not only are they well aware of the pitfalls of home alone online gambling, but they even embrace the luxury of self-indulgence it affords them to such a degree that they knowingly make poor decisions, in terms of both their play and money management.

It is true that B&M casinos have more than their fair share of poor decision makers and those who seem happy to execute rash, seemingly foolish wagers, but even these kindly contributors to the casino cause tend to have a modicum of self-respect and are aware of how they might be perceived by those around them – otherwise they might be tempted to make more rash bets and stupid wagers.

Yet put these same players at home, alone, moving around the cyber games under absolutely no scrutiny whatsoever, and there's a good chance they will indeed lose what they see as their inhibitions (but what we would simply refer to as reason), and with them more money than would be the case in a B&M environment. Playing blackjack in a closed room and with the table to himself still leaves the wayward player with the dealer as an audience, witnessing every mistake and poor play. But without such scrutiny the 'boring' nature of the game's long-term, Basic Strategy can be dispensed with online.

The embarrassment factor is of even greater significance with poker, where table image can be of paramount importance to the game itself and acutely humiliating for players. Online, however, the player's anonymity brings license to try out anything, safe in the knowledge that – other than a few comments in the accompanying chat box, to which if we so desire we can be blissfully unaware by simply switching the facility off – we are immune to abuse.

Virtual Chips, Real Money

In B&M casinos chips are used instead of money but at least there is an actual (physical) transaction taking place before play begins. Should these chips be lost, then the process begins again and serves as a reminder to the player of what is happening to the bank roll. On the internet, however, in order to replenish the stocks we simply make a few mouse clicks and continue where we left off. In virtual casinos it is significant that we don't actually handle the chips and are therefore not being constantly reminded of their very real part of our real environment. The downgrading of the cyber chips to two-dimensional status in turn serves to downgrade their importance to the player, who becomes used to interpreting this representation on the computer screen more as points than hard earned money.

Don't Drink and Gamble

B&M casinos are notorious for tempting their customers into drinking alcohol while they play, bringing drinks straight to the table and even giving them away on the house (how generous). Of course any serious player should refuse the temptation, while online gamblers are even better placed to avoid handicapping there play. Nevertheless it is not unusual to see the chat boxes in online poker rooms, for example, feature comments from players that they are drunk and, while this can be a crafty way to fool the opposition, it is also quite true. Once again one of the key attractions to online gambling is that we can totally relax in our own environment in a way that is hardly possible in a B&M casino. Indeed drinking and gambling are often grouped together by the uninitiated as tandem vices and the 'leisure' online gambler might well partake, but don't be surprised to see this combination prove damaging to the long-term health of the bank roll. Note that while some games require little or no analysis, concentration or even thought, it is still possible to go seriously wrong when making decisions regarding bet sizes and so on, while a couple of key strokes or unintended clicks of the mouse can easily lead to a $1 bet turning into $111... You've been warned.

Sleep

If you feel tired (or unwell) – don't play. Again this is glaringly obvious, but you'll see what I mean...

Chapter Three

Casino Games

For the traditional B&M casino patron one of the main attractions of actually going to a casino is the social aspect, something which is rather lacking in online casinos. It is evident that for online gamblers – other than those who enjoy the experience in the company of others – this element is not so important, which will have some effect on game selection and how these games are approached.

As is the case with a B&M casino, online we are invited to play slot machines, video poker, poker, blackjack, roulette, craps, baccarat, keno, Sic Bo, bingo and others.

Other than keeping a close eye on your bankroll, a priority when venturing into the world of online gambling that should always run in tandem with the aim of winning money is to enjoy the time spent on the computer. With this in mind I can only recommend finding the games that most satisfy your personal criteria and trying out a few sites until you find a couple that offer the best overall gambling experience.

Were this a book claiming to make you a casino winner, at this point it would be time to present clever sounding systems framed around the usual casino games. Fortunately I am interested only in providing a guide as to how we can get started and subsequently find online gambling an entertaining and, perhaps, a profitable time. Consequently I will not try to convince you that there is a magical way to overcome the house edge present in almost all these games for the simple reason that I don't believe this to be the case. That's life. However, we will investigate how the house advantage in blackjack – essentially a game of both chance and skill – can be kept to manageable levels (poker is dealt with in Chapter Four).

32Red.com casino lobby

Craps

Personally, I would only touch games such as craps, for example, with a view to achieving nothing more than having a good time and maybe striking it lucky before the house edge manages to eat its way into my bankroll. Craps has an array of wagers from which to choose, and these even include house edges as 'low' as 1.4 per cent on don't pass or don't come (1.41 percent on pass or come) and 1.52 per cent on place bets on 6 or 8, while buying/laying odds further cuts into the house advantage. However, these are the 'serious' player's bets which also require a certain level of both bank roll and patience that would be better exploited elsewhere. The other wagers are more fun but have prohibitive house edges of up to 16.67 per cent.

Roulette

Perhaps the most 'romantic' and exciting of casino games, roulette is what we tend to see in the movies, with fortunes won and lost at the spin of the wheel. With so many betting options and such a busy table the game also looks good on screen, being quite an entertaining and popular way to try our luck online. There are a few important attractions from the customer's perspective, the most important being that it is rather easy to play, with no need to invest time and energy learning the complicated strategies that might be appropriate if we are to improve our chances of success with some of the other casino games. We can simply place our money on the chosen bets and wait to see what Lady Luck has in store. Depending on our budget and how long we intend to play, the host of betting options affords considerable flexibility compared with Blackjack, for example. Going for glory with a bet on a single number can be a relatively inexpensive way to try for the 'jackpot' – albeit a little boring, perhaps, while the even-money bets such as red or black and odd or even lead to more wins but at obviously single unit paybacks. As is so often the case the House edge is a major factor with roulette.

Online Casino Roulette

With the 38-number US wheel the house has a big 5.26 percent edge thanks to the zero and double-zero additions, while the 37-number European version is much more player-friendly as the house advantage is therefore reduced to 2.7 per cent. There is also the so-called *en prison* rule which allows the player, in the event of a zero coming up, to keep half the (even money) bet or, alternatively, let the bet ride on the next spin – effectively producing a possible 1.35 per cent house advantage. But this is where the 'good' news ends and, from a purely expectational point of view, we are dealing with generally poor odds for the player. Of course this is all relative given that it is what we are used to, and it is quite within the realms of possibility that we beat these odds, but making a habit of playing roulette should lead to only one long-term result – the wrong one. Nevertheless, if this is the kind of fun game you prefer to invest your bank roll in, then all that matters is that you are aware of the house edge and prepared for it to take its toll somewhere along the way.

Note that despite the relative simplicity of roulette it is worth spending some time taking in the layout and nature of the betting options before playing for real, so here is another example (like craps) of trying out the casino's 'play money' facility in order to become properly acquainted with how the game works.

Blackjack

Unlike roulette, for example, where luck is the major factor and – rather than actual skill – the player's 'ability' is measured purely on money management, blackjack is a thinker's game. Although we have no more control over what cards will come next than we do over where the ball will land to rest on the roulette wheel, here we have an incredibly useful factor in the information provided by the cards we (and the dealer) are initially dealt. Combine this with the various betting options available at this stage, and the very real skill factor assumes just about as much importance as the luck.

Despite its apparent simplicity blackjack is nevertheless a fascinating game, and is therefore popular with internet players who opt for the online casino experience. Many players who approach these games with the opinion that gambling is generally down to luck (a negative attitude, perhaps but not, in the main, an unrealistic one) are bound to lose in the long-run, but these players will have fun, might get lucky and tend to move about the casino(s) from one game to another.

But it is the more serious player who runs the risk of losing more money. Unfortunately, where there is an outlet for players to use their skill through making accurate decisions, there is also plenty of scope for us to make mistakes, which is why no casino operator will lose any sleep over the accumulated results of blackjack.

Of course even if we have serious hopes of ending a session of online gambling with a profit, the time spent in front of the screen should be stress-free and relaxing (fun). After a hard day at work, or if we are simply looking to wind down, then the situation is not necessarily conducive to consistently making wise decisions literally every minute. And even if we are genuinely trying, to achieve a certain level of play requires a certain

tain amount of effort and aforethought – and time. Thus the vast majority of players will, on average and after a sufficient period of play, come out at least slightly behind. The beauty of the game for the casino is that most of their would-be discerning customers believe they are playing according to logic and losing only because of the house edge, when the truth is that, collectively, incorrect play over many hands simply sends the money in the wrong direction. So many players are attracted to blackjack because of the near negligible house edge, but the way the game tends to be played considerably accentuates the casino's advantage.

This book is a guide to online gambling and not a 'how to win' manual, and there is certainly nothing wrong in either playing these games for the thrill of it or trying out strategies in a game that involves little risk compared with almost all the others we are presented with (as long as this is done within sensible limits, of course). However, those of you who prefer to approach blackjack with a view to at least minimising errors might consider some kind of strategy based on certain established fundamentals.

Online Casino Blackjack

With so much literature and facts and figures on the subject so readily available it is not too difficult to find something that suits and, since we are talking about real money here, I would recommend putting some thought into the game rather than treating blackjack as a game of chance or attempt to reinvent the theory. Thanks in the main to computer simulation programs that have played out literally billions of hands, the correct strategies regarding the relationship between the player's cards and the dealer's up card (and doubling, splitting etc.) are now well documented. It pays to study these, but nowadays you can simply have the relevant tables in front of you (such information is even allowed in a B&M casino), while online gamblers can also take advantage of hints provided by the casino itself.

By using sound basic strategy alone we are able to significantly reduce the casino's edge to a fraction of a percent.

Blackjack Basic Strategy

The house edge in blackjack, 5.58 per cent, comes from a combination of two factors, the most important being the fact that with the player copying the dealer's 'forced' strategy (typically hitting a total below 17 and standing on the rest) the likelihood of this or that total being reached on either side of the table is (obviously) the same, but whenever the player busts he loses. This house advantage is tempered to some extent by the 3-2 odds paid on (uncontested) blackjack.

Fortunately for the player the otherwise significant house advantage begins to further fall thanks to the choices he is offered and that are not available to the dealer. For example just by electing to stand on any total between 12 and 17 when the dealer shows a low up card already reduces the 5.58 to 2.38, while introducing the facility to double on certain totals, split pairs, re-split and so on brings the player's disadvantage down to practically negligible levels.

Consequently, given these comparatively favourable circumstances for the player it seems appropriate to single out blackjack for further, albeit limited, consideration in terms of finding a sensible approach to playing online. This is where *Basic Strategy* comes into play, whereby the player uses a set of guidelines to help steer through the blackjack jungle, thus avoiding sometimes unlikely hazards that befall most players, including the well intentioned, independent yet – ultimately – consistent losers.

Don't forget that it is absolutely imperative to avoid drifting away from the basic strategy if we are to maintain an acceptably level playing field – experimenting or going against tried and tested practice to 'spice' up a playing session serves only to swing the balance very much back in the casino's favour.

Remember, too, that like any other casino game we should remember to adhere to general rules such as limiting and monitoring the bank-roll or the amount of time for a single session, stopping when tired and so on. But with blackjack requiring a certain level of concentration – at least if our chances of success are to be kept to a maximum – it makes sense to be extra vigilant. The effects of alcohol or tiredness, for example, are obviously going to make a bigger (negative) difference to blackjack results than would be the case playing the slots.

Below are some helpful hints based on Basic Strategy play (assuming multi-deck game where the dealer must stand on soft 17; reference to a 10 includes picture cards). Being able to refer during the game to any useful notes we make is obviously an advantage of playing online, as is not being pressured by other players and spectators who are prone to having an opinion on the correctness of your play.

Pairs: To Split or Not to Split

That is the question. The answer depends on which pair we have, the dealer's up card and the facility to double after splitting, but is fairly easy to get to grips with. In the case of aces, for example, regardless of the dealer's up card, and even taking into account receiving only one card per ace, it makes sense to have two lots of 11 at our disposal rather than one bite at the cherry with 2 by leaving them together. It goes without saying that 10s are best left untouched, 20 being too good a hand to mess with. Similarly, with a pair of 5s a Basic Strategy player should automatically never split as 10 is a good foundation hand which also has doubling potential (see Totals, below).

Another automatic Basic Strategy choice is to split 8s because 16 is a particularly unhealthy total and should therefore be avoided if we have the opportunity to do so – irrespective of what the dealer shows. If this is a 6, for example, splitting the 8s is the correct option because the odds are favourable compared with taking the 16, after which we are caught between a rock and a hard place. Against a 10, meanwhile, we are not too happy either way, but splitting is still the lesser evil even if this runs the risk of a double loss, as 16 versus the dealer's 10 is simply too big a handicap in comparison.

The following guidelines on whether or not to split pairs are just that – guidelines. Different game rules and conditions might mean tweaking them a little but, in the main, these are what I would consider part of Basic Strategy:

Aces	Always split.
10s	Never split.
9s	Split when the dealer has 2 to 6, 8 or 9. Otherwise, stand when faced with a 7, 10 or Ace.
8s	Always split.
7s	Split when the dealer shows a 2 to 7.
6s	Split when the dealer shows a 3, 4, 5 or 6. If post-split doubling is allowed split 6s when facing a 2.
5s	Never split.
4s	If doubling after splitting is allowed it is desirable to split 4s when the dealer shows a 5 or 6. Otherwise don't split.
3s and 2s	If doubling after splitting is allowed these pairs should be split when the dealer shows an up card from 2 to 7. With no post-split doubling split only when the dealer shows a 4, 5, 6 or 7.

Totals

The general conundrum blackjack players face is what to with awkward looking totals and awkward looking dealer's up cards, a typically agonising decision being that which features two poor hands that could feasibly bust. To add to the confusion there is the usage of the ace as 11 or 1, giving us so-called hard and soft totals.

Hard Totals

A hard total is a hand which does not feature an ace that counts as 11. For example a 10 and 7 combine to make a hard total of 17, whereas a 6 and ace make soft 17 (i.e. 17 or 7). Hard total situations are much easier to handle than those featuring soft totals (see below) because the prospect of going bust tends to rule out taking another card when the total is too close to 21 for comfort. Of course life is never easy, particularly when money is concerned, and the process is not automatic.

Let's have a look at how Basic Strategy points us in the right direction regarding hard totals:

17 to 21	Always stand.
13 to 16	Stand if the dealer's up card is from 2 to 6 inclusive. Hit if the dealer's up card is 7 or higher..
12	Stand if the dealer's up card is 4, 5 or 6. Hit if the dealer's up card is 2 or 3, or 7 or higher.
11	Double down in the case of all up cards other than an ace. Hit when facing an ace.
10	Double down in the case of all up cards other than an ace or a 10. Hit when facing an ace or 10.
9	Double down if the dealer's up card is from 3 to 6 inclusive (hit all other times).
8 or less	Hit.

Soft Totals

There is a little irony in the term 'soft' here as the element of danger to the well-being of the one's bankroll is ever present. A soft hand is one which includes an ace with dual values of 1 or 11, the point being that drawing a card on 16 soft, for example, cannot bust the player.

Alas, with the flexibility of choice comes the greater opportunity to make the wrong decision, so this particular situation is worth giving extra thought as here the benefits of adhering to Basic Strategy are especially relevant.

Obviously with 21, 20 and even 19 the hand is too good to be messed with. However, while 18 also seems a very favourable total, the crucial factor is the dealer's up card which, perhaps surprisingly, is more significant than many players might think. Those who follow their own, personal 'basic' commonsense strategy might automatically stand on 18 as they would with 19. This is in fact the wrong move when the dealer's up card is 9 or higher. When facing a 2, 7 or 8 it is correct to stand, while against 3 to 6 it is time to be aggressive and double.

17 is another soft total that can lead to trouble in the long-term if treated incorrectly. Being afraid to break an ostensibly decent total with a hit is illogical because standing will win only if the dealer busts, while hitting involves no risk and introduces the possibility of improving. 17 should always be hit, and the only decision concerns whether to double (if possible). The same goes for soft totals of 16 down to 13.

19, 20 or 21	Always stand.
18	Hit if the dealer's up card is a 9, 10 or ace. Stand against a 2, 7 or 8. With a three (or more) card total stand against 4, 5 or 6. With a two card total double down against 4, 5 or 6.
13 to 17	Always hit with three or more cards. With a two card total of 17 hit against a 2, or a 7 or higher. With a two card total of 17 double down against 3 to 6. With a two card total of 15 or 16 hit against 2, 3 or a 7 or higher. With a two card total of 15 or 16 double against 4 to 6. With a two card total of 13 or 14 hit against 2, 3, 4 or a 7 or higher. With a two card total of 13 or 14 double down against 5 or 6.
12	This, of course, consists of a pair of aces, which should be split at all times.

Card Counting

A number of online casinos offer minimal penetration in that they actually deal a couple of their decks, although dealing out two of eight decks, for example, hardly seems generous. So while in theory it is possible to derive something from this limited card counting online, it is far from practical because in order to cope with the fluctuations it would be necessary to have both a larger bankroll than is the case in a bricks and mortar casino and, of course, to spend more time playing.

One 'advantage' of blackjack online if you do give card counting a go is – unlike the real world (unfortunately) – being able to cope with negative decks by simply exiting the game and then returning, thus re-starting with a fresh shuffle. Nevertheless, the genuinely skilled card counter is better off finding his way to a real casino.

Slots

The results being pure chance, virtual slots present the online gambler with a sight and sound experience that keeps returning money to the player in the form of mainly modest wins and constantly promises the possibility of massive gains for relatively tiny stakes. With payouts that in the long-term earn the casino a few cents for every dollar wagered (see below) the player's main decision revolves around what kind of slot fits the bill and, this being a cyber casino, the better operators at least make sure to provide a rich variety of games to suit all kinds of slots fan.

Payouts

For most players sitting down at their computer for a couple of hours or so to wind down after work with a session in cyberspace, the big prizes are elusive. Instead the player is content to catch modest wins, while Lady Luck might occasionally show a bit of compassion and serve up a juicy combination of symbols, sights and sounds that result in a hefty boost in the credit box.

In the long run, however, slots take in more money than they give out, and we can find out this ratio by referring to the payout information that operators make available on their sites. (If they don't I suggest you look elsewhere).

RNG

The payout is determined by the RNG – Random Number Generator, which essentially generates results randomly from a known yet astro-nomical pool of possible outcomes. (We can argue all day about the 'ex-tent' of this computer generated randomness, but it is random enough for me...) By dividing this number of outcomes into the total sum of money on which they are paid out, we get the payout of the machine.

From a quick survey of online casinos we will see that, typically, the pay-out for this or that casino's slots might be around 95%, for example. This effectively means that, in the long-term, for every $100 invested the pay-out will be $95, and subsequent loss of $5. But how long is the long-term? And what happens before we get there? Whilst trawling through gam-bling forums I saw many virtual slots players complaining that they had joined an online casino after seeing payout claims of 98%, for example, only to play for weeks and suffer a payback that was much lower. What they failed to appreciate or acknowledge is that these are computer pro-grams we are talking about and, as we should be aware, computers deal with very large numbers indeed. Therefore, during the course of the long period at the end of which the payout figure will eventually be estab-lished just about anything can happen, with the short-term results capa-ble of large swings either way. Another, happier player might well report that she joined a casino to play the slots and after a few weeks has seen her bank roll snowball thanks to a payout way above the one she had seen advertised.

Remember that while the total possible outcomes are known, their distribution is random (that's the point), so what is not known is the timescale of the process. Furthermore, the computer is charged to merely throw out random combinations and is therefore not privy to the current state of play in terms of the payout ratio thus far. Consequently – and contrary to the claims of the non-believers – the program does not allow for the tide of slots results to change in order to 'even' out the payout.

Expect the Expected

The nature of random results, obviously, is to make each new spin of the reels a new and mysterious experience. We don't know what combination of symbols will line up next. Who's to say it won't be a winning spin, perhaps even the jackpot? Nor can we rule out a losing combination, or a whole series of them. Suffice to say, anything can happen, although, in the long-term, we can indeed expect the expected in that the overall flow of cyber dollars that passes to and from the customer and the online slots providers will eventually favour the latter.

One-Click Bandits

In the meantime, by joining a reputable casino with a wide range of slots on offer and reasonably high payout figures, you might consider putting, for example, $200 aside to try your luck and hope that the initial swing is in your favour. This seems like a decent bank roll considering there are penny slots available, but be warned as to the speed with which it is possible to play. Even at a B&M casino we see people race through hundreds of spins an hour, and online it can be even faster. With thousands of online players watching literally millions of virtual spins on any given day, that theoretically long-term payout is collectively bringing home the bacon at all times for the operators so that, with each spin you play, you are effectively adding a few cents of each of your dollars to their coffers.

Personally I find this long-term inevitability rather off-putting from a value point of view, but I appreciate the thrill of a big win and the fun factor, although lengthy sessions of slots also seems somewhat monotonous.

Of course as I write these wise words someone somewhere will be jumping up and down at home, spilling their drink and oblivious to the fact that – as is the wont of many an online gambler – they are dressed only in their underwear, yet tens of thousands of dollars the richer after sitting through thousands of spins of the jingling jangling virtual slots experience...

Strike it Lucky

Just as the occasional bricks and mortar slots jackpot winner generates great publicity for the casino that is paying out, online firms have latched on to the potential rewards of generating high payout so-called progressive jackpot games.

With a network of slots across a number of internet casinos it is possible for players from different sites to collectively boost a jackpot to a high level which, when it reaches $1 million, for example, prompts more players to join in the fun and thus contribute further. And so the cycle continues, with portals directing players to big, big prizes via more and more online casinos, every minute of the day. Someone eventually wins the jackpot, the media jumps in and throws amazing facts and figures to the public regarding the growth of an apparently happy internet gambling family and – on cue – consequently these casinos see a new influx of clients. Because a number of new customers will eventually do more than just play the occasional slot machine, the whole concept of progressive jackpots is a winner.

Always Look on the Bright Side of Life...

Meanwhile, those yet to strike it rich tend to remain positive in their quest thanks to the morale boosting wins that they hit. And herein lies the wonderful, almost hypnotic psychological effect of the slots (and video poker). By including in the many possible outcomes of the RNG software a vast range of winning combinations of varying values to the player the operators are able to help distinguish any thoughts of giving up the chase by virtue of the fact that a win – albeit perhaps rather modest but enough to add to the player's bank roll – is sure to come along sooner or later. This provides a well-timed reinforcement for the player and in doing so maintains interest. Remember that such winning combinations are random, but sufficiently numerous not to take too long in coming. The intermittent incidence of returns results in what is referred to as 'schedule-induced' behaviour from the player, not unlike addiction. Furthermore, combinations that can have the same kind of reinforcement effect on the player – yet at no cost to the casino – are those that feature big prize symbols in non-winning positions, serving to create a feeling of a near miss. Remember this the next time you feel like a break from your slots adventure. The jackpot is just as near or far away, irrespective of any recent wins – so take that break.

Bonuses

Everything has a price, including money. One key factor that helps fuel the online gambling explosion is the ostensibly generous bonus offers to new customers, the promise of free cash designed to ultimately secure your custom for the long-term, well after the necessary conditions to actually collect the bonus have been met. Unfortunately it is these conditions that are the downside to the special offer, with a minimum deposit being required and then a minimum amount to be wagered before the cash gift is yours. Typically, a bonus that matches a new membership start-up deposit of $50 might require the customer to wager 20 times the bonus amount. Now, depending on which games you play (bets on the 50-50 chances like roulette's odd/even or black/red do count) and how well you play them, there is a good chance that by the time you are ready to get your cyber hands on the $50 bonus you will have recorded a greater loss, and it is this zero expectation that effectively negates the bonus.

Some bonuses are better than others, with less stringent conditions, but it would be foolish to 'expect' a profit. However, while it is easy to criticise these bonus schemes, I would guess that lots of gamblers who are simply letting off steam play through considerable amounts anyway and are happy to see some returned. Meanwhile, there is now a facility available with online casinos that uses software that will optimally play certain games for you if maximising your chances is a priority.

More recently a new angle on the bonus scheme was introduced by **VIP-casino.com** in an effort to attract those potential customers unimpressed with the 'zero bonus' phenomenon. The firm has come up with a Cash Reward program that offers players a 1% reward on their accumulated net monthly winnings and 10% back on their monthly net losses, a realistic system which I suspect will grow in popularity amongst players.

Trends, Patterns and The Holy Grail

Venture into a typical gambling discussion group or forum on the internet and you'll find hordes of gamblers espousing the magical properties of trends and complex patterns of numbers and results in games of chance which, if sufficiently appreciated and properly acted upon, will reward the faithful with bags of cash. Much work needs to be done and eyes must remain peeled at all times but, when a pattern emerges it is time to strike, using flexibility and timing to make the hit.

These numbers-oriented gamblers are poles apart when it comes to their betting strategy in response to distinct patterns. The Believers will react to three consecutive reds in roulette by interpreting this run as a wave upon which they believe they can jump and subsequently surf their way to profit by betting on red coming up a fourth consecutive time. Non-Believers take the opposing position and bet against red on the next spin in the belief that all such runs come to an end sooner rather than later and black, therefore, will be next up.

Ironically, while sitting in completely opposing camps, both players' strategies are nonetheless fundamentally linked in that each takes a specific stance regarding the relevance of the trend or pattern itself.

Alas, at the risk of sounding like I need converting by the trend lobby, I should point out I believe only that each such result is purely random. And I recommend the reader approach roulette and other games of chance in the same way. This is true of traditional and online casinos, but especially in the latter case, where random number generators are in operation.

With some gamblers 'random' is almost a dirty word that threatens to undermine the work and energy put into going through charts, spreadsheets and related systems. Accepting the true nature of the randomness of casino games of chance might make spending money on 'how to win' books seem rather futile (or even foolish), but we might just have to acquiesce to the hard fact that the casino's edge is based precisely on any given likelihood being completely random over time. Perhaps I am wrong, and there is a Pattern super being out there somewhere doing favours for those in the know, but for the time being I must concur with the casinos, who tip the scales in roulette (if you will) in their favour by craftily adding a green zero or two to the 36 red and black numbers, thus serving to occasionally add insult to injury in the case of both aforementioned groups of Believers and Non-Believers.

To say that random means exactly what it says on the tin – that each new 'result' is completely independent of the last – is a simplistic way to describe this aspect of gambling, yet it is an easy statement to make if we don't subscribe to the theory that a trend or pattern has an influence on what will happen next. Feel free to gamble as you please, but using past events to help predict future events in games of chance becomes a serious commitment when money is involved.

You will notice when playing online roulette, for instance, that the results of previous 'spins' are posted on the screen. What are we supposed to do with this information, I wonder, if not use it to steer us in the right direction when making the next bet? I would suggest that following these past numbers should be for nothing more than adding to the entertainment, serving only to demonstrate the very unpredictability of random events. Eventually a pattern is sure to appear, of course, followed by another pattern, then another, then another...

That's life. Accept it, and gambling should prove far more enjoyable and much less frustrating.

Chapter Four

Poker

It has been estimated that around 20 million people play golf in the US, which helps explain why it is so popular on television. Recent attempts to estimate the number of US poker enthusiasts suggest the figure is anywhere between 50-100 million. Read on...

Once it was established that the online gambling industry was a potentially very juicy area in which to be involved, online casino operators looking for a new angle saw what might be done with player-to-player online gaming. This phenomenon has been most profitably manifested in the form of internet poker which, since around 2000, has emerged as a massive market, with poker websites quickly generating enough custom to give the more traditional online casinos more than just a run for their money and subsequently prompt the injection of more resources into this specific area.

Other than the 'adult' industry, online poker has – in just a few years – become arguably the fastest growing sector on the internet, and the pattern looks set to continue if recent developments are anything to go by. Poker's surging popularity has reached such a high level that in June 2004 it was one of the most searched for subjects on the internet. The top 10 search items on the global internet group Lycos's search facility for the week ending June 12th, 2004 saw poker ranked seventh, a little behind Britney Spears (4th) and two places higher than Harry Potter! Among the most popular poker related searches were online poker research, poker betting tips and Texas Hold' em poker.

The Online Poker Revolution

The beauty and subsequent popularity of online poker is the practically universal simplicity of its rules and the fact that it is recognised for one reason or another as the planet's most popular card game. On the one hand poker is easy to learn and easy to play, while on the other it is almost impossible to master, providing the enthusiast with thrills and spills (and the occasional win) along the way.

There are numerous versions of poker, but the game of choice that has become the universal form of the big tournaments is Texas Hold 'em. This might sound a little frivolous but it is in fact a very serious, logical game which, thankfully for all those involved, is deceptively simple. Here's how it works:

Each player is dealt two cards, face down (known as the *hole* cards). Five more cards, dealt face up, are the community cards. The first three are dealt together (called the *flop*), then comes the fourth (the *turn*) and finally the fifth (*river*) card. The betting takes place at each of these intervals, and players can use any five of the seven cards to make the best hand. And that's it.

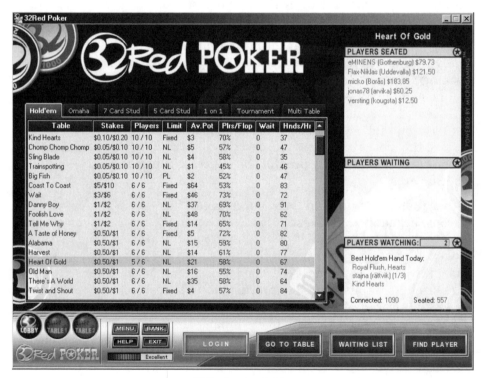

32Red poker lobby

The Attraction

The world of internet poker provides a medium in which players can test their skills against other poker fans across the world at very low or very high stakes, depending on bankroll and skill level (note that these two factors are not necessarily linked!), with enough table and tournament formats to cater for everyone. Add to this the 'chat' facilities at the virtual tables, countless special events and the prospect of winning riches for tiny initial outlays of $5 or $10, throughout the day, every day of the year, and it is not surprising that at any given time tens of thousands of players are battling it away online. And many, many more are joining them.

The $$$ Explosion

In 2002 online poker sites raked in estimated $200 million in commission revenue, a sum that represents total pot values of approximately $4 billion. These seem like very impressive figures considering the relatively short period of business but, with the online poker explosion expanding at a remarkable rate even as you read these lines, the 2002 takings are dwarfed by today's revenue. Moreover, when industry commentators heralded online poker in 2003 as the next big thing they were a little off the mark – it is even bigger than that.

There are two chief ingredients in the concoction that is poker's world conquering recipe – television and the internet. Only a couple of years ago, with 'live' action sport enjoying more and more air time on our television screens, the notion that televising poker would catch on with even a modest section of the television viewing public seemed optimistic at best. Yet in 2003 poker was very quickly becoming cable television's success story thanks to the Travel Channel's launching of the World Poker Tour. The use of cameras that give the viewer a sneaky peak at the players' hole cards, combined with snazzy graphics and facts and figures, created a viewing sensation not unlike live sport that was easy even for the hitherto non-poker acquainted audience to follow and to enjoy.

Incidentally, I should point out that, in the UK, Channel Four Television had already been successful in broadcasting poker with its excellent Late Night Poker series. Not only did this pioneering competition attract some of the world's top players (Phil Helmuth, for example), but using cameras under a glass table was, in my opinion, preferable to the later WPT coverage. Hosted by Jessie May, Europe's 'voice' of poker, these series did a great deal to popularise poker in the UK (and Europe) as early as the 1990s, long before the television fuelled craze started across the Atlantic, which helps explain why so many of my compatriots in some respects had a head start in terms of their online experience by the time the online poker revolution really began to take shape a few years later.

Of course, as with many worldwide phenomena, the USA's contribution ultimately had the greatest significance. From an initial audience of 790,000, WPT viewing figures rose this year to well over 1.5 million, and the new breed of poker fans can't get enough. WPT creator Steve Lipscomb predicts this figure will double by 2005, and this could well prove to be a conservative estimate.

On the strength of the Travel Channel's success, ESPN got in on the act with coverage of the 2003 World Series of Poker tournament, a re-run of which attracted almost 2 million viewers when it aired in the first half of 2004!

While television provided a perfect medium through which the uninitiated could be introduced to poker, with the Travel Channel, ESPN and Bravo (cleverly throwing the sure-fire element of show business into the mix with Celebrity Poker Showdown) producing a number of episodes of big money, high-roller, high tension drama for audiences to lap up, an outlet was needed through which we could actually play ourselves, and what better than the convenience and anonymity afforded the amateur (and expert, for that matter) by the internet.

There's No Business Like... Show Business Poker

During my time as a professional chess player I was also involved in organising and promoting international tournaments, and prospective sponsors would be at their most interested when they heard about which famous people were keen chess players. Movie idols John Wayne and Humphrey Bogart were reportedly quite serious, while modern day sportsmen are also spellbound by the game. For example the boxer Lennox Lewis, who succeeded in becoming the undisputed world heavyweight champion, once played a challenge match against former several time world snooker champion (and world class pool player) Steve Davis on primetime UK television. There are numerous other famous sporting and Hollywood celebrities who take chess seriously and, funnily enough, F.I.D.E., the World Chess Federation, once tried to exploit the potential razzmatazz by holding the World Championships in Las Vegas in the 1990s.

But more recently it is the poker boom that has created a rather sizeable following amongst major celebrities on both sides of the Atlantic – hence Bravo's Celebrity Poker Showdown, for example, from which there seemed no shortage of well-known poker enthusiasts from whom to choose. Challenge TV hosted their own UK version.

Ironically, from my side of the ocean, poker seems to have raised the ante, as it were, in the celebrity stakes, and stolen most of the publicity pot from chess (there is, perhaps not surprisingly, a definite connection between the two games). Even the aforementioned Steve Davis, once the president of the British Chess Federation, is a poker convert of whom it has been suggested has an alternative profession in Texas Hold 'em. Already a regular in serious television poker tournaments, he has also found success on the European tournament circuit. Furthermore, and mirroring the power of word of mouth that has helped swell the ranks of internet poker in general, other world class sportsmen are now part of the (internet) poker phenomenon, with snooker player Jimmy White winning the strong 2003 edition of the Ladbrokes Poker Million in London, Phil 'The Power' Taylor, arguably the greatest ever darts player, taking his fearless approach to the poker table and former international soccer player Tony Cascarino getting in the money on the European circuit.

Those of you familiar with either international poker or award winning UK television will have heard of Ross Boatman. One of Europe's leading poker players and part of the feared Hendon Mob along with brother Barny, Joe 'The Elegance' Beevers and Ram 'Crazy Horse' Vaswani (the last named-being one of the leading money winners during the whole of the 2004 World Series), Boatman made an interesting career change a few years ago when he switched from starring in UK television dramas such as London's Burning to becoming a very successful professional poker player.

All-In with the A-List

If celebrities have helped attract newcomers to poker, then the internet card rooms owe a very big favour to Hollywood star Ben Affleck, who is perhaps the most high profile celebrity poker player. In the first half of 2004 he became the first film star to win a major open poker tournament when he outlasted a field of 90 players in the California State Poker Championship, held at the Commerce Casino, the largest poker casino in the world. The hefty $10,000 buy-in made for a bumper prize fund, culminating in Affleck – who won an Academy Award for penning the screenplay to *Good Will Hunting* with friend, fellow actor and – alas – fellow poker player Matt Damon – collecting $356,400 for first place. Of course this is no small potatoes even for the likes of the Hollywood big hitters, but also at stake was a seat at the prestigious World Poker Tour Championship in 2005.

The actor outlasted a field of 90 players, including Tobey Maguire (star of the *Spiderman* movies), who went out the first day of the three-day tournament. Affleck had the second lowest chip count when the final table's nine players first got together. Among those he eventually knocked out were former world champion John Esposito and well-known poker professional Stan Goldstein, who finished second.

I wrote that Affleck was the first film star to win such an event because there are easily enough others to entertain the prospect of another major tournament falling into celebrity hands. Mimi Rogers, for example, is a well respected player who competed in the 2004 World Poker Championship in Dublin, while Lou Diamond Phillips, James Woods, Jack Black, Daniel Baldwin, Mena Suvari and Lolita Davidovich are just a few of the names to join Rogers, Damon and Maguire (and even Mickey Rooney) in the ranks of the serious poker player. Many of these celebrities gain valuable experience in the same way the rest of us do – racking up the hours on internet poker rooms, and some are even happy to do so under their own names or are happy to make their alias public knowledge.

So, with the Hollywood elite, sports personalities and others who enjoy the trappings of fame are investing time and energy on internet poker, not forgetting a handful of your workmates, a couple of your friends, your cousin, the postman, bank manager, butcher, baker, candlestick maker, tinker and tailor, then why not join in... and (hopefully) help relieve them of their cash.

Healthy Competition

Theories that internet poker would eat into the business of B&M casinos that host poker have proved incorrect, as the overall poker explosion has simply created a situation in which both newcomers and the more experienced, existing players number so many that there is great demand for the facility to compete in either environment. Moreover, the online poker sites in which can be found the new breed of internet enthusiast serve as an ever-increasing reservoir into which B&M casinos can tap for more clients, with online poker rooms organising their own so-called satellite events from which their customers can qualify for big money land-based competitions.

Money Makers

Step forward none other than Chris Moneymaker, the marketing team's dream online customer. By investing only $39 in his quest to qualify via such satellites on **Pokerstars.com** for the 2003 World Series finals, the Tennessee accountant (age 27) shot to stardom when he emerged victorious in the final 839-player field (each player with a theoretical buy-in of $10,000) to take the $2.5 million first prize. The fact that he succeeded at all was enough to champion the cause of internet poker, but being called Moneymaker led to a level of media exposure that propelled him and the game itself into orbit and served to inspire the 'average' man and woman in the street to join online poker websites with a view to emulating his success (or at least to somehow share in it).

This new influx of would-be money-makers led to more poker websites and further liaisons between internet and B&M tournaments, culminating in the 2004 edition of the World Poker Series attracting 2576 entrants and thus generating an incredible prize fund of around $25 million! To put this into some kind of perspective, scour the sports pages of your daily newspaper or surf the sports websites and then compare this figure with the money on offer for world championships of established leading sports... then the people power of (internet) poker is more readily apparent.

Not only was the record World Series field greatly boosted by the modern internet poker community (according to a WSOP spokesman more than a third of the players earned their seats in the World Series championship by playing in online tournaments) but, once again, the 2004 winner, Greg Raymer, a lawyer from Stonington, Connecticut who pocketed a nice, round sum of $5 million for his victory, qualified on the internet. As did the runner-up, David Williams, a junior economics major at Southern Methodist University in Dallas, who had to settle for $3.5 million (yet again **PokerStars.com** proved to be the 'lucky' site). With more internet qualifiers among the other 224 prize winners (minimum $10,000) we can only expect more of the same in future editions.

Juicy Stakes

Not so many years ago only a handful of poker websites provided a player-to-player facility, their customers perhaps numbering several thousand. I recently visited the excellent **Pokerpulse.com**, a website that constantly monitors the activity of online poker rooms across the internet. The fact that a website devoted exclusively to the progress and player traffic and so on of these online poker operators exists at all is indicative of how quickly the terrain has changed.

Now I can peruse a list of more than 200 (and rising) online card rooms, their accumulated active players at any given time amounting to tens of thousands (...and rising). And while you're mulling over that, according to **Pokerpulse.com**, during a typical 24-hour period over $90 million is going backwards and forwards across these virtual poker tables.

Money Rakers

While the player is happy with his or her opportunity to win money from other players, the online poker firms themselves have hit upon a reasonably risk-free environment in providing player-to-player (P2P) poker. There are two main reasons for this:

1. The players bring their own money to the tables.

2. The players pay a commission to the website.

In other words, other than the costs involved in the upkeep and so on of the service, those lucky, lucky website people don't even have to put up the cash. There are – as in life – winners and (many more) losers, and both sides of this gambling arrangement are effectively sponsored by the players themselves. The websites are in the middle, effectively providing a virtual meting place, for their troubles collecting a rake on a pot (the rake is much smaller than in a B&M game) or, in the case of tournaments, a modest fee on top of the buy-in.

There are cases with big promotional, multi-table tournaments that the operator guarantees a minimum prize fund which is ultimately less than the total buy-ins, but these nevertheless serve a purpose in terms of attracting and keeping clients.

Branching Out

As one would expect, then, online casinos and bookmakers have expanded by getting in on the act and introducing their own poker sites (typically by securing a deal with established software providers). In doing so they are able to exploit what is effectively a ready-made client base by converting a number of their existing customers who are (hopefully) happy with the present service, perhaps offering loyalty oriented bonuses to compete with the sign-up bonuses of rival sites. I recently received an email from Betfair, for example, urging me to try out their new poker site, their logic obviously being that those interested in a betting exchange are at least as likely to be interested in venturing into online poker as anyone else, and therefore willing to give them a go. Given that, as a member of Betfair, virtually all I have to do is download the software, I'll probably join.

And herein lies the beauty of adding a poker site to an online casino – the ability to both increase a client base while holding on to customers so that they don't jump ship and go somewhere else. As well as keeping casino players who will join the poker revolution, providing P2P poker also works the other way round, attracting new customers to the poker website who can then be invited into the casino proper. By doubling the services and facilities on offer the operator should benefit from the accompanying expansion, this being a standard industry move. All of this is clearly very good news for the players themselves, who are able to weigh up the pros and cons of a sizeable selection of websites and choose what best suits them.

Online or Bricks and Mortar?

While the people have spoken as far as the general argument is concerned, poker has specific issues to consider. Of course there are pros and cons with either scenario. For example some players might argue that if the opposition is easier to beat in B&M poker it is worth the inconveniences involved, while traditionalists believe that poker is not poker if not played in the flesh.

Ultimately even the most modern advocate of the online format could find himself venturing into B&M territory at some point in his career, as the connection between online poker rooms and events and their B&M brothers fuses in the form of 'live' events in which an increasing number of entries is made up of internet qualifiers.

Anyway, here are some points worth noting:

B&M pluses

Winnings can be collected on the day, which is not the case online.

The quality of the opposition is generally considered to be weaker at comparable limits than online. For example the typical 2/4 ring game on Party Poker – often recommended as a potential happy hunting ground for even the average half-decent player – has been equated with a B&M 4/8 game. If this is true on any given day, there is also the prospect in B&M of meeting 'tourists' and newcomers. These very inexperienced players – even complete novices – might usually spend their time at the roulette table or the slots, for example, and simply fancy trying their 'luck' at the poker table for a while. It is not unusual for such tourists to be content (even expect) to lose money as part of the overall gambling experience. This tends not to be the case online, where some effort is required before sitting down to play, and the emphasis is, in the main, to win money.

Tells: although there are internet-specific tells, there is opportunity for traditional poker tells to be exploited at a B&M casino. Of course this could prove to be a double-edged sword if you find yourself being read by the opposition.

Being conscious of other players' attention might help better focus our attention on the game. Internet poker, on the other hand, affords the player the often unhelpful opportunity to be distracted – watching television, surfing the internet, eating, drinking, venturing away from the computer between hands to look for more food and drink, listening to non-poker playing spouses' numerous requests to do 'little jobs' like changing the baby's nappy, unblocking drains etc., carrying out said jobs and so on are just a few of the possible distractions for the online player.

The hours spent in play can be more enjoyable thanks to the social side of B&M poker. Online there is only the chat facility.

No 'all-in' abuse (deliberately disconnecting to use a 'lifeline' to stay in the pot without having to make further bets).

No infuriating disconnections or technical/hardware faults that tend to arise online just when you're moving in for the kill (usually after investing heavily in the pot and after running out of all-ins!).

Online pluses

As well as the time and expense involved in getting to and from a casino, for those players fortunate enough to live within (convenient) travelling distance it is not always possible on arrival to find sufficient players for the kind of game you prefer, not to mention multi-table tournaments. Game (and opponent) selection is an important factor, and flexibility might not be an option for the B&M player. Online poker is available all day, every day, wherever you live. Thanks to the internet poker boom it really no longer matters what time zone you live in – there are always enough players.

Even after waiting for and being given a seat at a B&M poker table the conditions might be far from ideal for one reason or another. For example your neighbour might be the kind of person you would normally cross the street to avoid. He/she might be offensive, aggressive, loud, not a great fan of personal hygiene or even a thief. Seating arrangements might leave you short of necessary elbow-room or general comfort, while the room could be too hot, too cold, full of smoke etc. Online players are in control of their own conditions.

The combination of removing the physical aspects of the game (dealing, collecting cards, the movement of chips etc.) and introducing time restrictions makes for a much faster game online (thus allowing the player to be more patient). Furthermore, there is the facility online to play more than one table simultaneously.

Despite this option for online players to switch from table to table the rake is still lower than with B&M, where tipping is an additional cost. (Experienced online players might try to introduce their own, tip-free, waitressing service – in an ideal world provided by a spouse...).

Other than 'internet' tells there is no need to worry about our body language and general reactions to events when playing online. Not having to be concerned with traditional table image allows us to better concentrate on the game itself.

Finding a Site

In terms of individual sites and the number of players who frequent them the big hitters are **PartyPoker.com** and **Empirepoker.com** (who share customers), while **PokerStars.com, UltimateBet.com** and **Paradise-Poker.com** can also claim to have an impressive client base.

I can recommend any or all of the above for different reasons, as well as a number of others, but everyone has a favourite and mine is 32Red (**www.32redpoker.com**), which succeeds in more aspects of online gambling than most.

We saw in Chapter One how often lesser known countries provide licenses and play host to internet casinos, and 32Red, with a poker room and a casino (both can be found at **www.32red.com**) has an advantage over many of its rivals through its association with the UK by virtue of being based in Gibraltar. This reputable jurisdiction already instils confidence, and it is also reassuring to know that 32Red's founder and CEO, Ed Ware, is a former Managing Director of Ladbrokes International whose keen interest as both a casino and poker player manifests itself in the running of 32Red. (The online gambling industry holds such great promise to new operators that by no means all who jump on the bandwagon are either sufficiently experienced or even entirely capable of running a player/customer-friendly operation.)

It is interesting that, during the course of writing this book, I noticed how 32Red – which has been in existence for only a couple of years – endeavoured to maintain a high standard for its customers (the player volume is increasing by 15% per month and rising) by enhancing and adding facilities. One feature of internet poker, for example, is the ability to play on more than one table simultaneously, a practice that can prove awkward when the tables overlap on the screen. 32Red accommodated this increasingly popular trend by introducing a useful mini-view option which downsizes the tables so that they can be viewed simultaneously (my monitor is nothing special and I can have four tables running in full, clear view; how successfully I can play so many games is another issue entirely).

As I mentioned earlier there are numerous poker sites worth trying out. However, with competition taking its toll even on some of the more established operators (who seem to have over-played quantity at the expense of quality) it pays to give credit to sites that, in carving out a niche for themselves, are more than capable of fighting for and maintaining a share of the market. 32Red, for example, has persevered with a friendly and able customer service, fair and reliable games (the software partner is Microgaming), safety, security and quick payouts to customers – all qualities that one would expect from an online operator but which are actually in need of considerable improvement in the case of some big name sites.

Moreover, having tried out so many sites, those which succeed in passing my own personal test have become increasingly conspicuous in their quality and therefore deserve my time. Those sites which best meet the criteria in terms of what the player wants will benefit most from the online gambling explosion, as will the players who recognise and subsequently patronise them.

Prima Poker

One of the attractions of 32Red and a number of other online poker rooms is that it is part of the Prima Poker family. Like all good ideas, the concept that led to the creation of Prima Poker is simple and effective. As I mentioned earlier, for the very big poker sites it is normal to see thousands of players at their real money tables at any given time, thus guaranteeing continued profits in rakes and fees and keeping the proverbial fire burning. While it is true that everybody and his dog seems to be joining an online poker room (we all know that dogs play poker – I've seen that famous picture...) the competition to enrol each of these new converts can be intense considering the number of sites now in operation. Consequently the average site might occasionally lack the necessary traffic to hold on to its players, who might find themselves waiting too long for action. In fact this problem has in a way been compounded by the very success of poker, as newcomers (as well as experienced players) demand more multi-table, bigger volume tournaments that promise bigger prizes.

Online Poker Tournament

Prima Poker (powered by Microgaming software) was devised in anticipation of this phenomenon, the idea being to create a strong poker network by bringing together a few dozen sites from around the world in order to offer their collective players the opportunity to always find action.

Uniting players in this way, effectively forming a cross-casino community, allows the player to compete and communicate with players from a range of other sites. Consequently, by being part of an expanding network, a site is able to not only hold on to existing clients by providing them with a large pool of players and a regular schedule of multi-table tournaments, but the added dimension attracts new members. And all the time each site is free to nurture its own brand and site specific features and qualities while contributing to the community as a whole which, as word spreads and stand-alone sites fail to deliver, itself continues to grow. As the network grows, so do the frequency of events and the level of the prize funds, and the cycle continues.

The Future

What I find particularly significant is the actual volume of poker's coverage in the media, something which bodes well for the future. While there is clearly an element of luck in poker, serious players nevertheless tend to take the position that any kind of success in poker is essentially derived from the game's skill factor. While not necessarily distancing themselves from gambling (in my experience poker players have a penchant for – serious – blackjack), the distinction is there to be made.

For those in the poker industry it is important that poker is viewed in this way, as a mental sport with similarities to chess, for example, but in which money is used to keep score. Add to this the everyman, universal appeal, with movie stars playing alongside housewives from the other side of the world in internet poker rooms, and we can expect poker to be afforded an increasingly mainstream status that should transcend any debate surrounding gambling. In fact the fantastically positive flavour of the way in which poker has been treated by the media is also to the benefit of (online) gambling generally, with the sporting, competitive, fun factor adding a new dimension to what some might believe (unfortunately) to be the potentially unhealthy environment that is traditional gambling – the same suggestion might once have been directed at poker but that is hardly justifiable today, so the overall industry might well be the ultimate winner.

I predict that poker – particularly the attraction of online poker as a gaming pastime – will be the gambling industry's new 'face' that will act as a portal through which newcomers to gambling in general will find themselves taking a sideways step into good old-fashioned casino and sports book gambling.

Only time will tell and, should I invest another chunk of my life in an online gambling book in a few years, it would be nice to recall these words with a generous helping of self-satisfaction...

Chapter Five

Odds

Going Metric

A bookmaker or layer uses odds to express the price of a particular competitor to achieve a specific result in an event, such as the price of a horse to win a race, Tiger Woods to win golf's US Open or a woman to win television's *Big Brother*. Each selection in the market is assigned odds that reflect, albeit not purely, the bookmaker's opinion as to how that competitor will perform.

The traditional way in which odds are given is in the form of a fraction such as 10/1 (or 10-1), which essentially means that the theoretical probability of achieving the desired result is 1 in 11 (see Probability, below). If we bet £1 on a horse in the Derby at odds of 10/1 and it wins, then we collect £11 (the original £1 stake and £10 more for winning the bet). A big favourite, on the other hand, might be 4/7 (known as '2-1 on' – see below), requiring a wager of £7 to earn a profit of £4, while a bet of £1 here would result in a profit of only £0.57.

Because online betting is available to enthusiasts all over the world and not restricted to 'old-fashioned' UK punters, a popular and logical means of expressing odds is by converting them to decimals. This is betting's equivalent of introducing metric where once only imperial measurements existed, and it is indeed logical to break down what can be awkward looking odds to a single number, 4/7, for example, being 1.57. Note that in decimal form – also known as digital odds – this number represents the total return, including the stake, so here a (winning) bet of £1 at odds of 4/7 returns a profit of £0.57 plus the original stake. Ironically the strength of traditional odds in the UK is such that experienced punters prefer to stick with the familiar 2-1 (3.0) or 8/13 (1.62) rather than deal with decimal odds. Fortunately the internet firms offer their customers a choice as well as a facility that converts odds from one format to another.

An *odds against* bet is when the profit is greater than the stake, while *odds on* refers to a bet in which the money won is less than the stake. Some sports gamblers are attracted to bigger (longer) odds, with the prospect of considerable profit for little outlay, while others put more emphasis on a safer approach, concentrating on shorter odds betting in the knowledge that there is a greater likelihood of success but with smaller profits each time. Those new to sports gambling might see little long-term difference between the two strategies but (surprise, surprise) there is a bit more to odds than that, as we will see later...

The Bookmaker

As well as the UK's ubiquitous traditional high street bookmakers taking the necessary steps to keep up with the times and offer their services on the internet, the ever-expanding information highways that lead us to the gambler's virtual super-directory saw a surge of new bookmakers and sports books take their places in this enormous online industry.

With millions of customers around the world there are countless operators vying for their patronage, resulting in betting markets being created and competitive prices being offered for what we might think are obscure or dull sporting/competitive events. The bookie is simply in the business of making profits by maximising the number of bets taken across a range of events, throughout the day, every day of the year if possible. If something can be gambled on and the bookmaker believes there are enough people out there who might be interested in actually taking a position as to the possible outcome(s), then expect a market (a book) to appear. If it moves – they will open a book on it.

To achieve any kind of success the bookmaker must find a balance, offering sufficiently attractive prices to generate custom without actually being too generous (or wrong) in terms of how closely their odds on a particular outcome represent the realistic chances of that competitor's success (or otherwise), all the while seeking to maintain a balance in the book itself in order to avoid potentially hazardous liabilities. This juggling of different factors can be difficult to manage, which is why the operator makes certain allowances when making a book.

The Book

Unfortunately for the sports gambler, the bookmaker – being in the business of generating profit – must create a market in which it has the upper hand over those who are collectively betting against it. The internet might be described as a virtual world but, in the gambling industry, we must accept that the world of sports betting is very real and – from where the clients are sitting – slightly imperfect.

Let's take a look at an evenly weighted, 'fair' book on a horse race in which all five runners are equally fancied. In such a case the theoretical odds for each horse would be 4/1. Thus if we placed a wager of 1 unit on each horse the total outlay would be 5 units. Then, irrespective of the result, the winning bet would return 5 units – this being the original stake of 1, plus 4 for winning – and neither we nor the bookmaker wins or loses because 5 units have simply passed from customer to bookmaker and back to the customer.

Back in the real world, the odds offered by the bookmaker do not exactly reflect the true probability of a given outcome occurring. Just as a casino is willing to 'challenge' the customer only in games that have the odds weighted in its favour, so does the bookmaker endeavour to juggle the numbers accordingly. The actual probability of this or that outcome is indeed taken into account, and forms the first part of the odds making process. In order to help stay ahead of the game a bookie will employ the services of specialists who apply their expertise to assign odds to competitors and generate an initial market.

Continuing with horse racing, there are various factors that might be taken into consideration when compiling odds, such as previous results and performances of the horses (as well as anything relevant in the pedigree), jockeys, trainers and owners, the possible significance of the weather conditions (the going) at the race course and, when appropriate, the draw. The odds compilers use these to help in coming to a conclusion as to the *true* odds. Of course where the modern sports gambler has an advantage over his predecessors is in the ability to find the same kind of information, with no shortage of websites on the internet that specialise in all the facts and figures mentioned above. However, the bookmakers have the trump card by virtue of the fact that, after accurately (in theory) evaluating the true odds, they are then free to be literally economical with this 'truth' and go through the book with a view to trimming the odds.

Probability

It is useful when looking at odds to convert them to percentages in terms of the probability of each participant's (indicated) likelihood of winning, a true book's total sum of the competitors' percentages being 100%.

Calculating the percentage of odds can be done simply by dividing 100 by the sum of the two parts of the odds ratio and then multiplying the result by the second part. Thus to convert 3-1 we divide 100 by 4 (3 plus 1) to get 25 and then multiply by the second part, in this case 1, leaving us with a 25% chance of victory. Another horse could be 11-4, which works out at 26.67% (100 divided by 15 is 6.666, then multiplied by 4). To properly balance the book to 100% the sum of the remaining runners would therefore have to come to 48.33%, anything over being to the benefit of the layer, and a field totalling under 100% good news for the bettor, who could then back every horse and make a profit, whichever wins.

Over-round

While theoretically the total probabilities of all participants in an event must be 100%, it is clear that it is in the interest of the bookmaker to ensure that the total percentage comes to over 100%, which is where the so called *over-round* comes into play. The amount over 100% represents the bookmaker's profit, which is why it is quite normal to see over-rounds of 110% (a theoretical profit of 10%). Incidentally, the rare occasion when the total percentage is below 100% is known as over-broke.

The process can work as follows. Below is a table that illustrates how an odds compiler might produce a book on a six-runner horse race (or, indeed, any single six-competitor event) with the sole intention of producing true odds that are a good guide to the realistic chances of success of each participant. Note that the collective probabilities when converted from the odds total almost exactly 100% for this book.

Horse	True Odds	Probability (%)
1	2-1	33.33
2	11-4	26.67
3	4-1	20.00
4	6-1	14.29
5	25-1	3.85
6	50-1	1.96
Over-round		100.10

Looking at the over-round, the bookmaker would obviously not settle for a practically level book, so the next step is to produce a market more heavily weighted in the layer's favour by clipping the odds. The extent of these reductions vary with the circumstances, but even with minimal downward adjustments the over-round can change considerably, as the next table demonstrates:

Horse	New Odds	Probability (%)
1	7-4	36.36
2	5-2	28.57
3	7-2	22.22
4	11-2	15.39
5	20-1	4.76
6	40-1	2.44
Over-round		109.74

This time, despite the fact that each price has shortened, the odds have effectively remained the same in terms of the relative probabilities of winning the race. However, for the punter the price of taking an interest has just gone up (although the original prices would never have seen the light of day), and changes continue to be made as the bets start to come in.

The Market

Once the market opens and there is considerable interest for the horses, as the event draws closer successive visits to an online bookmaker to check up on the prices will see shifts in the market. Recommendations on sporting websites and in the media have an impact on the odds, while certain runners might attract a bigger than expected volume of bets for reasons that have nothing to do with the conventional factors that can be weighed up when making initial assessments.

The bookie wants to see money being wagered on all the horses so that, whichever horse wins, the over-round does its job and guarantees profit. However, such a perfect scenario rarely materialises, and it would be unusual for the appropriate distribution of bets to slot into place without the bookmaker having to tweak the prices in order to continually maintain a balance with the best prospects of profit. Therefore when a particular runner is the subject of much betting the bookmaker runs the risk of losing money in the event of that runner winning. When this happens the bookmaker reacts by shortening the odds on that runner in the hope that the latest, effectively more expensive price will be unattractive to bettors, who might instead seek better value in another runner, thus contributing to the bookmaker's cause for even distribution. Indeed to prompt customers into backing other runners it is standard practice to lengthen the odds of the market mover's rivals, whose consequent drift in the market can then be interpreted as a mere 'numbers' by-product of significant betting elsewhere in the market rather than a genuine reflection of its chances. In the meantime, any problems experienced in balancing the book can be countered by continually accepting bets on participants at lower odds than the 'true' ones.

Eventually, by the time the race is ready to start, the prices on offer could well be quite different to even the initial, doctored odds, being more of a record of the punters' betting. Perhaps I'm not being very kind to the bookmakers in the final odds table (below) because the over-round is hardly punter-friendly, but we can see that by retaining a flavour of the true odds the bookmaker can nevertheless generate a big swing.

Horse	True Odds	Probability
1	7-4	36.36
2	2-1	33.33
3	2-1	33.33
4	6-1	14.29
5	16-1	5.88
6	25-1	3.85
Over-round		127.04

Note that the 'outsider' tag of numbers 5 and 6 remains and, on the face of it, the prices look reasonable value. Yet, given that the odds compiler generally does a fairly good job in evaluating each participant's prospects, these latest odds are rather skinny in comparison to their more realistic prices in a fair book. Meanwhile, the odds for numbers 1, 2 and (especially) 3 have also shortened, but the changes in real terms are small compared with numbers 5 and 6. And herein lies an important feature of how the over-round manifests itself in the form of specific prices. Horse number 1 in this example, for instance, has shortened a little from a theoretically true price of 2-1 to 7-4, while number 6, the big outsider, was originally given a 50-1 price which now stands at 'only' 25-1. This is because the favourite's price, being already short, also remains indicative of its chances of success, whereas the originally big-priced number 6 left considerable scope for the bookmaker's margin. In engineering a juicy over-round the bookmaker concentrates on taking liberties with the outsiders' odds – which contributes more to the additional 27% here – and there tends to be little movement in the prices of an originally strong favourite. For those of you who are drawn to romantic long shots – especially where horse racing is concerned – the best place to look for prices are invariably person-to-person betting exchanges, where odds are set by individuals who – unlike the big firms – are not required to maximise the potential of margins by chopping up outsiders' odds (see Chapter Seven).

The Hunt for the Best Odds

Thus far the discussion of odds has revolved around the model of the traditional bookmaker's handling of the market, and how the existence of the over-round serves to make life that bit more difficult for the sports bettor. However, this is a simplified version of odds and betting and, fortunately, there is actually no such dark shadow cast over the punter.

Since the online gambling explosion has prompted the creation of countless online bookmakers and sports book operators, and since we are free to take our custom anywhere we please (in other words – anywhere that best pleases us), then from a bettor's perspective the market on any given event is not restricted to a single firm but is – thanks to the internet – a veritable mega store of prices.

This means that by comparing what is on offer across a range of bookmakers we should not have to fall foul of prohibitive over-rounds. Moreover, with so much sport and other bet-friendly events taking place (practically non-stop) across the planet there tends to be both a sufficient number of attractive prices as well as the occasional window of opportunity that can lead to guaranteed profit.

As I mentioned in the very first pages of this book, those adventurers with a certain convenience oriented confidence tend to be attracted to both gambling and the internet, the latter phenomenon being the perfect medium for just about all aspects of the former. Some sports gamblers are satisfied to take a position on an event without really worrying too much about the odds they take. For them the outcome is all that matters. Others might have an account with one or two favourite bookmakers or perhaps just a single firm that offers its customers other forms of gambling, such as casino games or poker (these are players who simply like to gamble).

But there seems little point in using the internet if we fail to avail ourselves of the fantastic facilities it has to offer, and with free bets and special offers for new members with just about every online bookmaker and sports book it makes sense to consider casting our own net as wide as is practical. In this way, by having more feathers to the sports betting bow, there are in turn more chances to exploit opportunities afforded us by competition (not forgetting genuine errors and poor predictions on the part of bookmakers). All we have to do is surf the internet, compare prices and investigate all the different types of market framed around this or that event, throw in a bit of experience and guile and put our money on the line reassured by the fact that we got some value. Easy...

Fortunately there is a facility on the internet that makes life so much easier for the discerning sports bettor who prefers not to blindly place a bet. Avoiding work doesn't necessarily make someone lazy and, with so much going on, any time saved can be profitably used.

Checking out the Odds

The internet seems littered with useful sites and services that cater for practically every imaginable interest or pastime. Many of these completely fail to deliver, many require that we hand over our money and most prove to be a bit disappointing, but some are a very welcome addition to our online Favourite Sites list.

For the more serious sports gambler – and we should all approach sports betting with at least some level of seriousness – one such indispensable part of the armoury is Oddschecker (**www.oddschecker.com**). As the name suggests, the site's focus is on checking out available odds for a given event, which it does by scouring the internet for the key players in sports betting and bringing prices and markets together, comparing odds in order to see which bookmakers offer the best prices. However, apart from being an invaluable odds comparison service, Oddschecker also provides useful information, guides and tools that help better equip the sports gambler – all completely free.

These sites are so useful that after availing myself of the services and assistance on offer from Oddschecker I can only marvel at the sports gamblers of old. One could argue that the internet bombards us with so much information that we can't see the wood for the trees, and in some cases this can indeed be a problem, particularly when much of this information is contradictory. But there are some things we certainly do want to be acquainted with, and the movement of – as well as issues related to – betting markets is right up there at the top of our priorities list. How other information and tools and so on are dealt with is up to the individual and the constraints of practicality, but the beauty of the internet is that the choice is nonetheless ever-present, with certain aspects of sports betting and gambling there to be investigated and utilised.

Fortunately for the bookmakers their customers tend to comprise of the following:

- Sports enthusiasts with limited experience or understanding of gambling
- Casual, hobbyist, fun gamblers
- Punters with an appreciation of the key elements of sports betting

Of course these are very simplistic representations but, essentially, most of the bets taken come from players in the first two categories, while a number of those in the third could definitely help themselves by investing a bit more time into their deliberations. In order to illustrate exactly what kind of useful tools can be taken advantage in the quest to make the most of our bankroll, below is a selection of the facilities offered by Oddschecker.

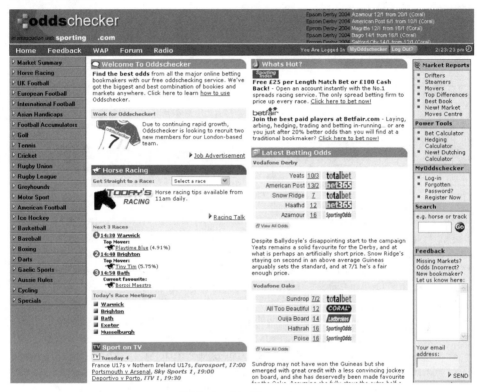

Oddschecker Homepage

As you can see from the site's home page it is possible to garner valuable odds and market information on sporting and other events from around the world. Selecting a sport from the left menu takes users to a more detailed sub-menu from which a range of different bets on offer from leading bookmakers for specific events can then be viewed thanks to a series of market reports.

For example in mid-May 2004 I wanted to have an overview of the odds for the outright win market for the summer's much awaited European Soccer Championships in which my beloved England had a fighting chance. Here is Oddschecker's table showing the prices available with a couple of dozen leading online bookmakers:

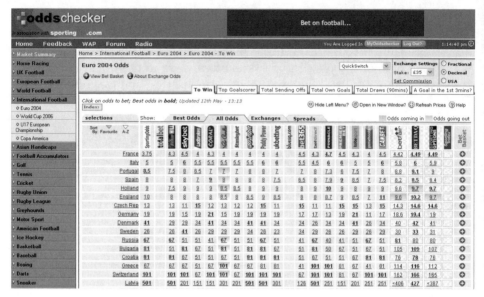

Euro2004 win market

Even a brief glimpse of the table, which features live (decimal) prices for all 16 teams of the final stages, is enough to demonstrate just how useful this service is. As for England, we can see that a fairly common price for their lifting the trophy was 8.0 with at least six or seven firms. Even if I were to scour the internet myself there is a good chance that after a few attempts I would be satisfied that this is a decent price (especially after logging on to the bookmaker offering a miserly 7.0!), whereas now I can get on with someone else at a better price, the highest – a whopping 11.0 – available from a firm I very much doubt I would have checked out were I left to my own devices. Meanwhile, traditional arch rivals Germany's odds range from 11.0 to 21.0, an enormous difference (considering the team's potential in these big events) that demonstrates the extent to which online firms can differ in their assessments and subsequent prices.

Now, having decided that I do indeed wish to add to the tension and inevitable heartache experienced when watching England's campaign in Portugal by backing up my patriotic, passion fuelled support with actual money, I can simply click on the best price of 11.0 or the bookmaker's logo at the top, whence I am automatically transported to the bookie's website. Not being a member of the very generous **canbet.com**, it is then a matter of registering, betting and waiting for glory...

Of course I would like to say that, as an avid and serious soccer watcher of many years, I mapped out the route of outsiders Greece to the final and helped myself to odds of over 100-1 to win enough money to take the Dunnington family on a luxury holiday. That would have been nice, but the

the only people going on holiday after Greece won the championship were the bookmakers, who must have been checking out possible destinations with each exit of a fancied, well backed nation... Nevertheless, with England performing well and reaching the quarter-final stage in good shape, anyone lucky enough to get the initial price of 11.0 would have been able to cash in by laying England on a betting exchange at much shorter odds (see Chapter Seven).

As well as the straight odds comparisons, there are other features of Oddschecker that delve into important areas. One such is *Best Books*, which gives the over-round for each event, while the following can also be found.

Top Movers

This report lists the latest movers for a single bookmaker in a market. For example, a runner might have shortened significantly from 9.0 (8-1) to 4.5 (7-2) with a particular bookmaker, while the best odds still available in the market are 7.0 (6/1). The report is ordered by significance, with a calculated value given to identify the significance of the move is. As I mentioned earlier the shorter odds tend to be more realistic, so a big outsider being cut from 100-1 down to 50/1, for instance, is less significant than a more fancied 6-1 runner shortened to 4-1. Top Movers are available for all sports (while ante post Top Movers are available for horse racing markets).

Top Differences

Listing the latest differences between bookmaker odds for the same bet, here we might see that a golfer, for example, is available as short as 34.0 (33-1) to win the US Open yet as long as 51.0 (50-1) elsewhere.

Steamers

Here a steamer is a selection that has shortened in the market from its opening price by more than two bookmakers. The Steamers report gives the best price available for the selection and the number of bookmakers it has moved with. As is the case with Top Movers, the report is ordered by significance. Such a tool is useful as it provides a good overview of where the money is being wagered on a particular event.

Drifters

The complete opposite of the Steamers report, this features selections that have lengthened in odds from the opening price (more than two bookmakers).

Spreads/Fixed Odds

With so many sports gamblers having been introduced to betting through the spreads firms (see Chapter Six) there is a tendency to deal exclusively with the new format at the expense of traditional fixed odds. While each is completely different it is obviously not the case that spreads are superior to fixed odds, or vice versa, and it would be wrong to ignore the options. Oddschecker has a facility which calculates and compares possible returns with each format for the same event.

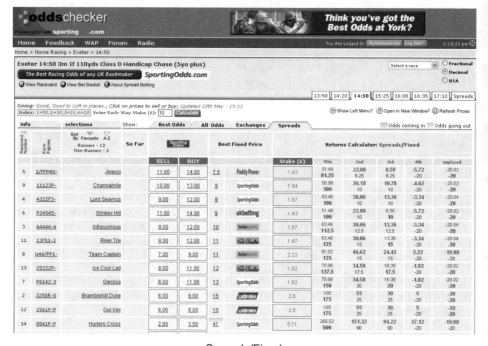

Spreads/Fixed

The table above uses a horse race to illustrate the difference in returns between spreads – paying out 50, 30, 20 and 10 points for 1st, 2nd, 3rd and 4th respectively – and the best available fixed odds for an each-way bet – paying the 1st, 2nd and 3rd – with a £10 stake (i.e. £20 wager). The figures in the Stake column represent the amount per point incurred in a *buy* on the spreads for a total wager of the same amount as the fixed odds bet – £20. For example risking £20 on a buy of Team Captain at 9 with Sporting Index works out at £2.22 per point. Therefore if the horse wins the return on the spread bet is £91.02 (50 minus 9 is 41, multiplied by 2.22), while the fixed odds bet at 11.0 (10-1) returns £125 (10x10 for the win, plus 2.5x10 for the second half of the each-way bet).

The Odds, They Are A-Changing...

With online bookmakers constantly altering their prices it is all the more important to take advantage of the services and snippets of analysis offered by sites such as Oddschecker, who keep abreast of these changes and update the markets every few minutes. You will see on these illustrations, for instance, that odds in blue are 'coming in' (getting shorter/lower) and those in pink are 'going out' (getting longer/higher).

Oddschecker also features a live 'ticker' that shows changes in online betting markets as soon as they are detected. As the site itself points out, the online bookmaker that offered the best odds as recently as five minutes ago may not necessarily be offering the best price now.

Covering all the Bases to Pocket Free Money

While a facility provided by a website such as Oddschecker to help us locate the best value is obviously very useful and saves a great deal of time and effort, the more alert sports gambler looks for even more than convenience. By investigating the prices on offer around the web for the different outcomes of a particular event it is occasionally possible to place a wager on each eventuality and guarantee a profit.

Let's take a soccer match as an example as there are so many matches throughout the world, throughout the year, that there is almost always sufficient interest to prompt numerous firms into offering prices on the result. And we don't have to be soccer fans to appreciate that the sport is an excellent source of opportunity.

The simple soccer market framed around the result obviously allows for three separate bets – home win, draw and away win. After scanning Oddschecker's prices pages we might find that different firms have quite different opinions regarding the likely result. The significance of such varied odds is that, with a combination of bets placed with a selection of firms, any of the three possible match results leads to profit.

Of course these possibilities don't present themselves so often that we can limit our action exclusively to helping ourselves to free money, and when they are there we need to find them. Here is an example of such an opportunity, with an explanation of how to go about determining the stakes.

Example

In a match between Brazil and Argentina the best decimal odds on each of the home win, draw and away win might be 2.90, 3.5 and 3.0 respectively. Note here that a bet of $1 at 3.5 gives a return of $3.50 in the event of a draw.

For a return of $1 on a home win we would have to wager $0.34 (1 divided by 2.90), while $1 returns on the draw and away win would require bets of £0.29 (1 divided by 3.5) and $0.33 (1 divided by 3) respectively. Thus to receive a payout of $1 regardless of the match result we would have to wager a combined total of only $0.96, this being $0.34 + $0.29 + $0.33.

Spoilers

Of course life is not that simple, and even if the winds of fortune seem to be blowing our way, there are other factors to consider.

1. In order to be ready to act quickly it is necessary to already have accounts with a number of bookmakers, something which in itself automatically ties up money that might otherwise be utilised elsewhere (and how many firms should we join if we are to maximise our chances?). Furthermore, each successful event results in a gain with only one firm, while losses at others mean these accounts need addressing.

2. Placing separate bets with three different firms takes time, and there is always a danger that after success with the first two, for example, the odds of the third might have moved in the wrong direction, resulting in a negative commitment.

3. Some firms don't take such single bets.

4. These calculations take into account expenses such as tax or commission that we might incur with some operators.

Know Your Odds

Being able to calculate odds and probabilities is one thing, but fully understanding even ostensibly simple odds is more difficult than some people believe. Numbers can be confusing at the best of times, but throw in the prospect of emerging from a bit of mental odds tennis with someone else's money in our pocket and judgement can easily become clouded, particularly when we are presented with odds that appear so basic we don't even bother questioning them.

Here's a good example of surprisingly deceptive odds that tends to fox the casual bettor. All we need are two kings and an ace from a deck of cards. Putting them face down, ask a friend/father-in-law/prospective victim to put his hand on whichever card he thinks is the ace. Then – without showing the cards – you take a look at the other two yourself. Of course there will be either two kings or a king and an ace. It doesn't matter, because next you turn over a king and put it to one side, leaving your friend's choice and the remaining card – one of which is the ace.

Then we come to the odds and the bet. Your friend now has the choice to go with his original selection and see if he found the ace, or instead try his luck with the other card. The vast majority of people in this situation would believe – quite understandably, given what looks like a very simple choice – that because there remain only two cards it doesn't matter which they go for as the odds are even. However, this is a big mistake, albeit a common one – even amongst those who might consider themselves knowledgeable gamblers. In fact, rather than facing a casual, lucky-dip even money bet, your friend is actually a 2-1 underdog while his hand remains on his original selection, while the remaining rejected card is a 2-1 favourite. If he believes his chances are 50-50 you can happily while away the hours by laying him odds of 3-2 that he's found a loser. How is this possible? Well, the point is that his logic is based on the fact that in this particular situation there is now a straight choice between two outcomes, either his card is the ace or the other card is, giving the card he's keeping a 50% probability of being the 'winner' of a two horse race. However, originally there were three 'runners' in the race, and the probability of each card being the ace was 33.33% which, in terms of odds, is 2-1. So the original selection was a 2-1 shot, and it still is! Your friend should always take the option of switching to the other card as sticking to the original selection means sticking with the original 33% probability of success. Meanwhile the remaining card has a 67% probability – in other words this remaining card will be the ace two out of every three games. Try it out yourself a few dozen times...

Chapter Six

Spread Betting

What is Spread Betting?

Not very long ago people who wagered on sports and other events were given more or less the same opportunities as earlier generations when, for example, race goers would pit their wits against the (odds) 'book' maker. In the vast majority of cases traditional sports betting consisted of trying to select from a list of participants which would emerge the winner, or amongst the winners. Despite the expansion of this or that market and the introduction of different types of bet to keep the customer interested, the world of betting had finite boundaries in which the customer was rather limited in terms of choice. The bookmakers offered markets based only on results and possible outcomes, effectively keeping winners (and payouts) down to a minimum. This was the set up for generations. Then *spread betting* came along, allowing the eager punter to win (and lose) money on just about anything and with – crucially – the actual result of sporting encounters being just one item in a mega store of betting opportunities.

Taking a leaf from the way standard financial markets work, spread betting presents the punter with the opportunity to bet on a 'spread' of numbers that relate to eventualities in a specific event. This could be the total number of goals in a soccer match, the distance in lengths between the winner and runner-up of the Breeder's Cup, the number of cars managing to cross the finishing line at the Monaco Grand Prix, the number of holes before Tiger Woods drops a shot at the US Masters... the list is endless.

How does it work?

The words spread and index might initially sound complicated compared with the simplicity of something being an evens chance or a 20/1 outsider, but the mechanics of spread betting are quite straightforward. Let's say a spread firm opens a market on the number of players to finish a tough golf tournament under par, the quote being 26-30. If you think the course and conditions won't be as tough as the market makers and that the eventual number of players managing to break par will be more than 30, then you 'buy', while if you think the lower end of the spread is in fact too high you 'sell' at 26. When making the bet the customer selects a stake per point (in this case a 'point' is a player finishing under par). This stake helps determine the extent to which the player wins or loses once the event has ended, being multiplied by the difference between the initial buy/sell level at which the bet was made and the actual final level (known as the *make-up*). The stake can be very low – 50 cents, for example – and therefore lead to very modest gains and losses, or high – $100 is by no means unusual – when the customer's liabilities can be considerable.

Imagine our golf tournament to be particularly difficult for Tiger and his fellow players, with only 10 succeeding in breaking par after four gruelling days – selling at 26 for $100 per point nets a big profit of $1600, calculated by simply subtracting 10 from 26, to leave 16, and multiplying this by the stake per point of $100. Buying at 30 for the modest stake of 50 cents per point would lead to a loss of only $10 (30 minus 10 leaving 20, and multiplying by 50 cents). But an unexpectedly easy tournament with a make-up (final result) of 50 players under par would tell a much different story, with the buyer now making $10 and the seller licking his wounds due to a painful loss of $2400 (50 minus 26 leaves 24, multiplied by the $100 per point stake).

Perhaps it is this 'facility' that spread firms provide to risk large sums of money, combined with the vast range and types of markets available, that causes the uninitiated to be intimidated by spread betting. For example when I approached a well-known men's magazine – which not only features sport but also predicts results – with an offer to write a gambling column, the editor was particularly confused by spread betting, saying he had heard that it was very complicated and that people seem to be able to lose lots of money. At the time I was a little surprised that an editor of a magazine aimed specifically at the very section of society from which spread firms receive so much custom was so unaware of his readers' considerable interest in 'modern' gambling, but anything new that comes along – especially in a world that has changed little for such a long time – is bound to be met with some sort of confusion.

Let's take the final of soccer's World Cup as an example, when a spread might be quoted on the total goals market of the Brazil-Germany encounter of, say, 2.9-3.2. If you believe that the match will be a tight affair with both sides putting safety first, then you 'sell' at 2.9, choosing your stake at, for example, $10 per goal. Alternatively, if you expect an open, attacking game, you can 'buy' at 3.2 for $10 per goal. Thus a final score of 1-0 would leave the seller in profit – 2.9 minus 1 leaves 1.9 which, multiplied by the stake of $10, comes to a gain of $19. The buyer, on the other hand, loses – 3.2 minus 1 leaving 2.2, multiplied by the stake per goal of $10 to result in a loss of $22.

Meanwhile, over at Wimbledon, the total games market for the men's final might be quoted at 35-37. Would-be tennis experts who predict a one-sided match and sell at 35 for $10 per game would then be in for a shock when the tense match becomes a marathon and finishes 7-6, 6-7, 7-6, 6-7, 15-13 for a total games 'make-up' of a whopping 80... this would make for an expensive final with a loss of $450 (happy buyers would pocket $430 with the same stake).

And this is where we see the potential volatility of spread betting compared with the finite format of fixed odds, where at least we know the extent of the possible loss from the outset as this is determined at the level of the bet itself.

Beware!

Spread betting must be approached with caution if we are to avoid trouble. The newcomer should become well acquainted with the dangers inherent in the unpredictability of the many components of this or that market, as well as the potentially hazardous outcomes that can materialise even when using ostensibly modest stakes. The general, fundamental gambling golden rule that we should gamble/play only with money we can afford to lose is an *absolute* priority here. In fact spread firms make sure to provide exactly this advice on their web pages, television 'text' pages and printed material in order to remind their customers not to get carried away with bets that seem simple when looked at in the context of fixed odds but actually leave bettors open to considerable losses. Sporting Index, for example, feature the following warning:

'Risk Warning – Spread bets carry a high level of risk to your capital. Only speculate with money you can afford to lose. Spread betting may not be suitable for all customers, so ensure you fully understand the risks involved and seek independent advice if necessary.'

Meanwhile, elsewhere I found more excellent advice:

'...you should not engage in this form of betting unless you understand the nature of the transaction you are entering into and the true extent of your exposure to the risk of loss. The amount that you may win or lose will vary according to the extent of the fluctuations in the price of the sports based index ('the underlying market') on which the bet is based instead of a pre-

*determinable sum when a normal bet is placed. For many members of the
public, these transactions are not suitable; you should, therefore, consider
carefully whether they are suitable for you in the light of your circumstances and financial resources.'*

Spread Betting Companies

Fortunately we are spoilt for choice when it comes to spread betting, with
no less than four firms vying to secure our custom – Spreadex, IG Index,
Cantor Index and Sporting Index. All tend to offer the same kind of markets and cover the same sports and events, so it is usual to have an account across the board for the sake of flexibility and the advantages that
competition bring the customer. However, while in these firms are practically identical when we look at the bigger picture, each has endeavoured
to carve out its own image, a specific flavour. All four are excellent, well
organised, client-friendly firms that go to great lengths to offer a vast
range of markets and prices.

As with anything else in life for which we must part with our money, it
pays to shop around – whether this be for the best value in the same market or the kind of betting format that most suits you. Over the years I
have been impressed by each of these firms for various reasons, but my
personal favourite is *Sporting Index*, from where examples of markets
and spreads and so on in the following pages have been taken.

Unlike traditional bookmakers, some of which are steeped in gambling
history, spread firms seemed to appear from nowhere in the early 1990s,
yet they soon established themselves as major players in sports betting.

To help form a picture of how spread firms have secured their place in
the world of sports betting here is a look at Sporting Index which, starting as they meant to go on, was founded on April Fools Day back in 1992.
In January 2003, in anticipation of the growing interest in their area of
the betting industry Sporting launched **BetHiLo.com** as part of its drive
to make spread betting more accessible. BetHiLo strips out all the jargon
associated with spread betting and enables punters to bet from as little
as 1p. Then in November 'Bet on the Move' was launched to provide mobile phone users with the first java enabled sports spread betting service.

Is your money safe?

Typically, Sporting Index is regulated by the Financial Services Authority (FSA), which is the British equivalent of the American Commodity
Futures Trading Commission (CFTC) and Securities and Exchange
Commission (SEC) combined. The FSA is the single statutory regulator
responsible for regulating deposit taking, insurance and investment business, and inspects spread betting firms on a regular basis to ensure that

that each firm conforms to the strict rules of the Authority. One such rule is the setting aside of funds as a guarantee against a company suffering big financial losses, while other strict regulations serve to protect the client. Consequently any money deposited with FSA-regulated companies is segregated under the Authority's regulation to ensure complete security, while winnings are also guaranteed under FSA regulation.

Online Security

Not surprisingly Sporting Index – like other spread firms – have designed their website with the security of customers a top priority. Secure server software encrypts all clients' personal information such as name, address and card number so that it cannot be read as it travels across the internet.

Facts & Figures

Sporting takes over 2.7 million bets a year. It is interesting that, although profit per bet is declining – which can, perhaps, be explained by sports gamblers in general having become better informed and more appreciative of what spread betting entails – the volume of punters using the services is increasing rapidly. The firm has around 30,000 clients, although by the time you're reading this there will be more converts to spread betting.

Not surprisingly, the company makes between 50 to 55% of its revenue from soccer.

At the time of writing as much as 60% of its business is conducted online, and I would expect this figure to increase significantly. Apart from the growth in actual numbers of customers leading to more traffic on the internet – whether they be those who already have some experience in sports gambling or those for whom their first foray is through spread betting – it is a fact nowadays that for so many people the web has become a more accessible, user-friendly part of life. Consequently, existing clients, with more time to use the internet and therefore able to look around a spreads website for information and prices and so on, are more likely to do their betting online, too. Meanwhile, spread firms themselves are constantly working to improve their sites and make them more attractive, easier to use and understand and, ultimately, easier to place bets on.

Novelty Markets

I must admit that one of the reasons I like Sporting has nothing to do with the vast array of markets they provide across major events. Rather it is the number of novelty markets on which the company prides itself that catch the eye. Some of the most famous have been: *Ronaldo's Girlfriend* (how many times she would be spotted by the television cameras during a World Cup Match with Brazil), *Sing With Pride* (how many players would sing their National Anthem on camera before the World Cup Final) and a market that was meant to brighten up Britain's Budget Day, framed around how many sips of water the Chancellor of the Exchequer would drink during his speech.

Those new to spread betting might wonder who actually decides to take a position on such eventualities, but however frivolous these gambling opportunities may seem, they are nevertheless indicative of the beauty of spread betting. Traditionalists might look down on this 'fun' approach, claiming that spread firms would create a market on anything as long as the event was guaranteed sufficient coverage to generate an interest. Indeed this is true, but gambling is gambling.

We could place a wager on whether a golfer will win a tournament or on when he first hits a double-bogey. Alternatively we could risk our money on an informed, well analysed prediction that France's top soccer players will be victorious over their rivals and emerge victorious after the final whistle of the World Cup, or we can instead invest our money by taking a position on a spread market concerning how many times these same players will kiss the bald head of their goalkeeper (for good luck, I hasten to add) during the same event. Either way, these two examples feature one conventionally sensible betting proposition and one silly option, yet all four involve having an opinion on the likelihood of something happening.

That these novelty markets should anyway be taken seriously because – regardless of their names and subject matter – they deal with quantifiable results is seen in the popularity of the *Magic Sponge* market which, for soccer's World Cup Final, for example, was framed around how many times the trainer would come on the field of play to attend to an injured player. Now the very same market has pride of place alongside the more traditional ones for major soccer matches. Moreover, thanks to those tireless statisticians who seem happy to accumulate and assimilate all sorts of ostensibly useless information, we now have at our disposal all kinds of facts and figures that, over time, can help in forming an opinion on even the oddest of betting propositions.

Chinks in the Armour

Followers of American Football will be pleased to know that this is the sport that was the cause of Sporting's biggest loss to date on a single event. The big day for punters was the 1998 Superbowl Final between Green Bay Packers and Denver Broncos. Sporting predicted that the Packers would win by between 12 to 15 points... the Bronco's won and cost the company over £200,000.

What's in it for them?

Unlike the traditional bookmaker, the beauty of spread betting for the firms is in the spread itself which – to a degree – is designed to please everyone. Using the total goals market in a soccer match as a typical example, quoting 2.9-3.2 gives backers a simple choice to make (higher or lower) compared with the equivalent bets available for the same market with a fixed odds bookmaker, such as (for example) 9/4 for under 2 goals, 5/2 for exactly 2 and 10/11 for over 2.

The spread here is the sports equivalent of being prepared to buy a stock on a financial market for 2.9 and sell for 3.2, the point being, of course, that with an equal level of buyers and sellers there is a guaranteed profit in the form of the spread. And the bigger the spread, the bigger the profit. If Mr Smith sells total goals at 2.9 for $10 per goal and Mr Jones buys at 3.2 for $10 and the final result is 2-0, then we have the following results: Mr Smith wins $9 (2.9 minus 2 is 0.9, multiplied by $10) and Mr Jones loses $12. Therefore the spread firm collects $3. If the match ends 0-0, Mr Smith wins $29, Mr Jones loses $32 and the firm makes $3, while a one-sided encounter ending 6-0 would leave Mr Smith out of pocket by $31, Mr Jones up $28 and the firm with $3.

By now the fundamental difference between fixed odds betting and spread betting from the perspective of the bookmakers should be apparent... The fortunes of the fixed odds bookmaker rely heavily on results, while the conditions upon which profits are based for the spread firm remain the same regardless of results – what matters in the world of spread betting is that the bookmaker must try to balance out buyers and sellers in order for the spread to do its magic. To some extent the fixed odds bookmaker both creates a market and subsequently becomes part of it, competing with its customers and preferring certain outcomes over others when watching an event. The spreads bookmaker, on the other hand, creates the market (an index) and then seeks to maintain a status quo regarding supply and demand, safe in the knowledge that as long as this is achieved then the actual make-up of the market concerned is irrelevant. Here the roll is to oversee and maintain the market which is being fed by – and is relevant to – only the buyers and sellers. Obviously this is in the spread firm's ideal world. In the real world, when betting constantly takes place during the event itself (known as *in-running* betting – see below) the market maker's task of adjusting an index is by no means automatic due to various factors in a game and uneven betting or heavy action in one direction and so on. Nevertheless, the main point here is the profit generated by the spread, whatever the result, provided the volume on either side of the spread is well balanced, which is why very large bets, for example, might sometimes prove problematic. Remember that the spreads bookmaker must continue to respond to the action on both ends of the index rather than look to join in with the buyers and sellers and take a position regarding results and outcomes. Of course the firm's original quote tends to be a more or less accurate appraisal arrived at by experts, usually based on hard facts and figures. As we shall see an index might be tweaked a little to take into account some of the public's more typical yet less reasoned betting behaviour but, in the main, the market is dictated by actual supply and demand.

Sporting Index Homepage

The Joy of Spreads

There are a number of attractions to spread betting that have revolutionised sports gambling and generated a whole new breed of modern punter. Indeed many of today's spread bettors have little or no experience in the traditional fixed odds field, which they might find old-fashioned, cumbersome and restrictive. Of course the fixed odds firms have done a great job in expanding their own markets, and with the two formats being quite different there is plenty of business to go around. This is because some types of sporting events and aspects therein tend to be more suitable in betting terms to one or the other, while in many cases there are advantages and disadvantages on both sides, and the decision to bet with fixed odds or spreads boils down to the individual's preference and factors such as prices, their availability, potential gains, liability and so on.

But spread betting is undoubtedly in front when it comes to flexibility in terms of the type and range of markets. Fixed odds, of course, are fixed, which both reduces the market maker's options and limits the potential interest for the bettor.

Betting In-Running

With spread betting – as is the case with financial markets – an index on one or more markets during the actual event itself is constantly updated, this so-called in-running betting revolutionising sports gambling by presenting customers with betting opportunities throughout a match, be it soccer, US football, tennis and so on. If an event is being shown live on television somewhere, there should be all kinds of markets available to satisfy sports bettors's appetites. There has always been great interest in live sport on television, but the considerable increase in its coverage and availability in recent years has resulted in new recruits to sports betting, due in no small part to the arrival of spread betting firms, whose no-nonsense formats and ever-expanding range of markets has succeeded in creating so much interest in live sport that television pundits now discuss the margin of victory in the run-up to (for example) an international rugby match, when in the old days only the result would be speculated on.

This fantastic flexibility was unheard of before the spread firms came along, earlier punters being restricted to placing bets only before play began or, when appropriate, during official intervals (e.g. half-time in a soccer match).

The facility to bet on outcomes during play proved so significant that over the least few years the fixed odds firms have also introduced in-running prices, although the very nature of the fixed odds format is restrictive in that both bookmaker and customer lack options compared with spread betting. Returning to the total goals market in a soccer match. a spread is much easier to maintain for both parties than are fixed odds. For example in the event of a goal during the opening seconds of the match the 2.9-3.2 spread – which, of course, would generally gradually drop as the match remains goal-less – will simply increase to 3.9-4.2, effectively changing little for those yet to get involved (the situation is not that clear-cut but, in order to make my point, it is simple enough). But with fixed odds the in-running process is much less clear and in fact rather cumbersome. Earlier we saw a typical example of the total goals prices that might be available to a fixed odds bettor before kick-off, namely 9/4 for under 2 goals, 5/2 for exactly 2 and 10/11 for over 2. Already there is a significant difference here between the two formats. Regardless of the customer's opinion on whether the match will be low or high scoring, there is the separate bet for exactly two goals to factor in. When the early goal is scored there will then be a new set of three quotes to get to grips with, with each new change in the score line bringing with it yet more new prices. Obviously these can be exploited to make a profit if the game is going in the right direction but, compared with the utter simplicity of the spread, life is far less complex following the logical movements of an index.

Closing Out

So, with a goal in our mythical soccer match being scored within the first minute the original spread of 2.9-3.2 is replaced by an updated one of, say, 3.9-4.2. Then, just ten or eleven minutes later, when the index has gone down a little to 3.5-3.8 (after taking into account how much of the full 90 minutes playing time remains as well as how the spread might best be balanced between buyers and sellers), a second goal doubles the lead to 2-0, at which point the index increases further to around 4.5-4.8, way above the initial quote. It is at this point that those who had bought at 3.2 are licking their lips at the prospect of making a quick and healthy profit here and now, thanks to spread betting's facility to *close out* a position.

This luxury is a hitherto unavailable possibility that highlights the way in which in-running spread betting has completely altered sports betting in favour of the customer. Had we originally bought at 3.2 for a stake of $100 per goal we would now seriously contemplate closing out. Note, incidentally, that such a bet would leave us open to a potential loss of $320 were the match to end without a goal being scored (assuming we stayed involved throughout). With the spread now at 4.5-4.8 we could sell at 4.5 for $100 per goal and net a profit of $130 – not a bad return after less than a quarter of an hour's play. Moreover, what we have here is a situation not dissimilar to the spread firm itself, for we have made a profit irrespective of the final result, the only important factor being the level of the spread. It would not be surprising for the match to drastically change course, with the team in the lead changing tactics with a view to keeping their lead intact, no longer seeking to score but concentrating instead on nipping in the bud any aggression by the opposition. Should this strategy prove successful the score line might well stay at 2-0 right until the final whistle. Now, buying at the beginning of the match at 3.2 for $100 per goal and subsequently letting the bet run through the duration of play would lead to a loss of $120, while closing out straight after the second goal would return a gain of $130. This is a big difference indeed. On the other side of the spread, sellers at 2.9 for $100 per goal might elect to close if the match remained 0-0 after 80 of the 90 minutes, at which point the index might be 0.4-0.6 (note the gap is 0.1 smaller now that most of the time has elapsed), buying for $100 per goal at 0.6 for a profit of $230. Here, too, others might prefer to sit out until the end when a make-up of zero would earn an additional $60, but this approach runs the risk of going pear-shaped in the unlikely – albeit quite possible – event that the closing minutes erupt in a goal-fest.

For the fixed odds sports gambler there is no way to so conveniently step out of the heat with no further involvement. Years ago the fixed odds bet would leave us locked in for the duration, relying solely on the final outcome of the market. While it is now possible to guarantee a profit or elevate the potential of the initial wager in response to an altered score line by making other bets, but the practicalities of carrying out such an exercise can be problematic at the best of times. Fool-proof closing out is exclusive to spread betting.

There are no definitive rights and wrongs regarding whether or not to avail oneself of the opportunity to close out in-running bets. Some players begrudge 'paying' the actual spread between buying and selling when closing out, while others are content to adopt a wait and see policy, accepting the risk involved in turning down a price that might not be reached for the rest of the event, but nonetheless hoping that this is not the case. For the more adventurous/ambitious/optimistic/greedy buyers the prospect of being on the right side of a thrilling, unusually high scoring encounter is too much to let go, even when faced with a guaranteed and quick turnover.

How we deal with closing out is irrelevant here; what matters is that it is an incredibly important option specific to spread betting, allowing the player to make a profit as long as the market goes in the 'correct' direction long enough to allow closing out. Furthermore, given that spread betting is also likely to inflict big losses even on the more experienced players from time to time, closing out is also a means by which we can cut (potential) losses when things are going in the wrong direction. Again there is more than one way to approach this scenario, with some people believing to ride out the storm and others adopting a safety first, live to fight another day policy. The choice is yours, but the choice is there! We should be very happy indeed to be presented with an option that allows us, for example, to actually make a profit during the running of an event when, ultimately, our initial judgement might prove to be way off the mark.

It's not just the winning that counts

While spread betting puts the customer in situations which can lead to substantial results-dictated losses (although it is possible to have a safety net in the form of a 'stop/loss' limit) the major attraction of spread betting is that the more right we are, the more we win. Being able to back up confidence in the actual nature of the outcome of an event – as opposed to the result – affords us the opportunity for bigger gains than would be the case with a traditional 'win' bet. For example, returning to Brazil-Germany, if you think Brazil are too powerful and will win easily you can bet on the *supremacy* market (the winning margin). If Brazil are the favourites this might be quoted at 0.4-0.7 (goals), so you buy at 0.7 for, say, $100 per goal. If you are correct and the final result is 4-0, then celebration is in order – 4.0 minus 0.7 comes to 3.3, multiplied by the stake of $100 per goal to amount to a profit of $330. A standard fixed odds win bet on Brazil would have returned the same profit regardless of the ease in which they won, whereas choosing the spread bet option rewards the punter for the degree to which his assessment is correct. A scoreless end to the match would lead to the buyer losing $70 due to the initial commitment of 0.7 of a goal, while a result of 0-4 would lose $470, highlighting the extremes involved.

It's not just the losing that counts

Spread betting also affords us the opportunity to oppose a favourite even if we believe that it will win. For example, were Brazil to play a friendly warm-up match before the World Cup against a team that is decent but nonetheless much lower in the world rankings in, then even the supremacy quote might be as high as 2.9-3.2, for example. Given that these matches can turn into no more than a bit of exercise for the favourites – who tend not to over-exert themselves or risk injury in the run up to the big event – while the underdogs do their utmost to put in a good performance, although we would expect Brazil to have little trouble winning, we could justifiably consider selling here at 2.9 goals. It is quite possible that the final result will be 2-0, 1-0 or 3-1 in the champions' favour, thus netting the punter a profit. Of course a whitewash would be bad news, but some spread bettors are content to oppose the favourites in this way if they believe the lower end of the quote is too high.

Stop Loss (& Stop Win)

A stop loss is a limit placed at the time of opening a bet on the maximum amount the bet can lose. This is used for those customers with certain types of account that stipulate setting limits to safeguard against big losses, as well as serving to restrict the liabilities of the spread firms themselves.

Playing the Markets

Not surprisingly there are seemingly countless markets, each with its won individual character. Before looking specifically at a few sports, here is a typical example of how it works.

Tournament Index

This is straightforward, with points awarded to competitors based on how they perform within an event. For example the tournament index for Wimbledon is:

Winner	100
Runner Up	70
Losing Semi-Finalists	50
Losing Quarter Finalists	33
Fourth Round	20
All others make up	0

To give you a good idea of the level at which quotes tend to be offered in the run up to such a major event, I picked out a selection of prices a week or so before Wimbledon 2004 was due to begin. These were (seedings in brackets):

Federer	(1)	56-60
Roddick	(2)	44-48
Henman	(5)	38-42
Hewitt	(7)	30-34
Safin	(19)	11-14
Ivanisevic	(-)	2-4

As you can see, supporting tournament favourite Roger Federer is effectively a prediction that he will make the final, for even if he lost in the semis he would in turn lose those 10 units for those who bought at 60 points. (I was 'lucky' enough to have picked up on Federer's potential a few years ago and duly bought him very cheaply, only to have the smug smile wiped off my face when he crashed out in the opener). Meanwhile Britain's would-be hero Tim Henman, who has reached the semi-final stage several times but not yet won a place in the final seems nevertheless fairly reasonably priced for buyers. Further down the list I saw Safin at 11-14 which, given that he is capable of beating anyone, would appear to be rather low, although before getting long with any player or team in a knockout tournament it is worth taking a look at the probable opposition. Ostensibly good value spreads that offer relatively low maximum losses might not look so juicy if at each stage there is a good chance the opponent(s) will be tough.

The market continued to change so that, two days before start of play, Federer's spread had risen four points to 60-64, Roddick and Henman each increased their stock by two points, Ivanisevic had remained at 2-4 and Hewitt buyers could save two points since his price was now 28-32.

Quite a few people must have agreed with my initial opinion that Safin's price was a little on the low side because during the same period the 11-14 quote had grown to 16-19, already enough of an increase to net those who had got long early a profit of two units. As for Hewitt, whose recent form was okay but not exactly confidence inspiring, perhaps the lack of buyers could be explained by the occasional mention in the media of his being knocked out in the opening round in 2003 by Croatian Ivo Karlovic when defending his title, earning the Australian the dubious distinction of being the first men's champion to do so at the first hurdle since 1967. Such snippets of information have a habit of dissuading punters from taking a position.

Note that it is not unusual to be able to positively close out before an event gets under way. In fact the more experienced spread bettors will take a special interest in competitors way before the markets are even published, weighing up which players or teams are likely to generate the most pre-tournament/match interest and therefore be the subject of size-able alterations in their price. The spread firms' own initial allowances for a patriotic surge of buyers can occasionally prove to be an underesti-mation, a media frenzy serving to send out 'support' signals to those who might otherwise not have placed a bet. The England soccer team and Tim Henman are two such examples. Conversely, cold-blooded sellers seek to exploit what they consider to be illogical, 'blind' buying by simply waiting for the masses to hike up a particular spread, holding out until the price looks to have peaked and then selling with a view to seeing the player or team make an early exit. Bookmakers' tend to be more susceptible to big-ger liabilities on events in which these patriotic bets are placed, hiking up the spread in order to compensate for the imbalance created by the hopeful buyers. Consequently it is indeed worth contemplating a sell in such circumstances.

Anyway, back to the Wimbledon Tournament Index, and on the morning of the first day's play the quotes for our selected players were as follows (price increase/decrease in brackets):

Federer	(1)	61-65 (+5)
Roddick	(2)	50-54 (+6)
Henman	(5)	42-46 (+4)
Hewitt	(7)	28-32 (-2)
Safin	(19)	17-20 (+6)
Ivanisevic	(-)	2-4 (=)

Notice that, other than Hewitt and the 'veteran' former champion Ivanisevic, we have significant increases in the quotes, three of which are more than the actual spread. So we can see how the market is busy from the minute the spread firm produce their prices and, just like a financial index, participants' stock rises and falls in line with demand and expectancy of future events – and all this takes place before play has begun...

Sports Markets

While the spread firms revolutionised betting by introducing respectable – even quite logical – index based markets on just about any (non-sporting) event that might generate interest and custom and therefore attract new clients, it is traditional sports and their components that form the backbone of spread betting.

Although some sports have more players, possible outcomes, playing time (and periods) and so on than others the nature of the spreads is such that there are enough markets with which to attract customers who might prefer a change of scene from traditional betting, where the single, fixed odds bet for a long-term event such as a tournament, for example, lacks the flexibility of taking a spread position.

This section deals with some of the possibilities available to the sports gambler interested in adding the spreads markets to his armoury. While this book is meant to be part guide, part taster for the would-be internet gambler, it is nevertheless worth delving into a specific area of betting occasionally in order to paint a more detailed picture of what to expect in various fields of online wagering.

It seems prudent to take a closer look at how different spreads markets can be used to help formulate particular betting methods and approaches that are specific to spread betting, and for this I have chosen golf as the feature sport. I have resisted the urge to use soccer (which we have already touched upon in previous examples) as the main feature because golf also enjoys popularity the world over, is easy to understand in that the object of the game is hit the ball into the holes in as few shots as possible and, importantly, is appreciated equally on both sides of the Atlantic.

Golf

Increasingly popular with all ages and in all walks of life, it is not surprising that golf is well catered for by spread firms, who have come up with a variety of markets. These range from an overall index for a tournament itself to markets that deal exclusively, for example, with how many double bogeys or worse will be made on an infamously difficult hole at a major event. Not only do the different types of market provide the golf enthusiast with interesting bets, but there is plenty of scope for the well informed sports gambler to turn effort and good judgement into profit.

Because spread betting is the perfect betting medium for the specialist, the nature of golf, with fields of around 150 players, is not easy for the market makers to get to grips with week in and week out. Sunday night sees the end of one tournament and by Thursday another begins, leaving the spread firms with little time in which to keep up with statistics, weigh up players' strengths and weaknesses regarding this or that course and so on and monitor other factors that might affect a player's perform-ance. Of course the quotes are created by experts who are used to closely following the sport, but they do have a lot of work to get through every week, and their experience doesn't preclude favourable opportunities for the well prepared. Furthermore, the set-up of golf tournaments, with 72 holes being played over a period of four days, affords us considerable flexibility when betting in-running. Remember that in-running bets here do indeed stay so for the duration of the event if we so desire, these mar-kets being updated at the end of each day's play.

Here are some examples of what kind of bets are available, based on the Sporting Index markets:

Tournament Index

This actually covers only a group of players who, for the purposes of this particular market, are involved in a tournament amongst themselves. The mini-tournament usually consists of 10 players, the idea being to predict how a player will perform in relation to the others named in the specified group. The beauty of such an index is that it provides an oppor-tunity to support players who you believe should perform well, but against a small field (rather than the old-fashioned fixed odds win or place bets that pit the player against 150 or so rivals).

The spread firms will select ten of the more fancied prospects to be in-cluded in the tournament index because they are guaranteed to generate substantial interest in the market. Within the index, points are awarded as follows:

1st	50 points
2nd	30 points
3rd	20 points
4th	10 points
All others	0 points

Thus in a typical US Tour event, Phil Mickelson might be quoted at 14-16 in a competitive 10 man index that might include other top ranked players such as Davis Love III, Ernie Els and David Toms, for example. If you believe that Mickelson will perform well in relation to the other nine players in the index, then you 'go high' (buy) at 16, let's say for $5 per point. If Mickelson does indeed finish higher than the others in the group he will be awarded 50 points, leaving a profit of $170, this being 34 (50-16) multiplied by the original stake of $5.

That would be good news, but the thing about such an index is that Mickelson need finish only 3rd of the group to earn 20 points and thus register a profit of $20. Remember that this is an in-running market, updated at the end of each day's play, so it might be possible to close out with a profit were your selection to get off to a fantastic start on the opening day or simply perform much better (or less worse) than his index rivals, in which case the spread might increase to 29-31, for instance.

As usual there is an element of risk with in-running bets, the nightmare scenario here after buying a player who then goes on to pull way ahead of the other relevant players being the possibility of disqualification from the tournament, for example, which would automatically result in a make-up of zero on the index. Nor is it so unusual for a player to be comfortably leading the tournament index after three rounds, perhaps with a price around 42-44, only to have a disastrous final day, falling behind four or five of the others. With this in mind, those players who get off to a poor start are sometimes so low on the index after the opening round that they might be worth a buy, given that players in these groups tend to be quality performers and are quite capable of recovering for the weekend's play.

As well as buying supposedly in-form players the tournament index also presents us with the opportunity to oppose those who we believe might struggle amongst a group of their peers. In such cases a well-known, top rated player given a fairly high quote of, say, 21-23 could feasibly become a sell in view of the fact that only two of the remaining nine strong golfers need to finish higher in order to guarantee a profit – whether (in this case) this be 1 (3rd), 11 (4th) or 21 units, depending on where the player finishes within the group.

The would-be shrewd sports gamblers who believe a particular well-known player to be struggling with form or consistency will refrain from selling their selection at the beginning and instead hope that he has a good opening day, the aim being to then take a position and sell when the quote has gone up, thus maximising potential profits should the original prediction prove accurate, and reducing the potential loss in case the player manages to find form throughout the remainder of the tournament.

It is theoretically possible for all players concerned to each have a terrible tournament and miss the cut. However, although they would no longer play a part in the tournament proper, the players' respective results would, from the point of view of the market, be equally relevant as was initially the case before a ball was struck. For example if Player A misses the cut by ten shots, Players B and C miss by fifteen, Players D, E, F, G, H and I are either disqualified or withdraw during the opening day, and Player J makes the cut, then the final make-up for these players is:

Player J – 50 points, Player A – 30, Players B & C – 15 points each (sharing the sum of 3rd and 4th places) and the zero for the rest.

Note that after making the cut Player J would finish first in the index even if he subsequently self-destructed and finished the tournament on twenty over par – as far as the index is concerned the tournament would effectively end once he becomes the only player to make the cut. However, if he were later disqualified, then his make-up would be zero, and the other players would be promoted.

Usually what happens in a tournament index is that after two rounds the group has been reduced to perhaps six or seven players due to missed cuts, with one or two just managing to scrape through to the weekend's play, a few doing reasonably well and a couple pulling away. These considerable differences in the fortunes of the players are then reflected in the quotes, in turn prompting some people into closing out their positions or having additional bets and others who have not yet got involved to jump in now that the field has been narrowed down.

The finite nature of this kind of group index makes having a position on a golf tournament a relatively easy, manageable exercise, which is why Sporting Index, for example, will have more than one so-called Super-10 index, each group consisting of similarly ranked players.

Although technically in-running, the fact that this market is suspended during the actual play can be frustrating. For instance if you watch play progress or follow the scores of the players in the group, what at one point are good results in relation to your bet – at which time you would like to have been able to close out – are quite irrelevant because only the scores at the close of play are what matter.

Leaderboard Index

Here the whole field counts, so the quotes are lower and the rewards greater. While every player still involved in the event is theoretically part of the index, as the name suggests, only prices for those currently on the leaderboard are quoted, spreads being updated and new prices appearing as play progresses and the leaderboard changes.

Typically, the Leaderboard Index might have around twenty players at the beginning of the tournament, with the following scoring system: 60 points for 1st, 40 for 2nd, 30 for 3rd, 25 for 4th, 20 for 5th, 15 for 6th, 10 for 7th and 5 points for 8th.

This time Mickelson might be quoted at 10-13, so if you thought he was going to do well he would still have to finish at worst in the top six places of the whole tournament in order for you to make money (assuming you don't close out at some point). Notice that a buy at 13 would result in a loss of 13 times the initial stake per point were Mickelson even to play very well throughout the whole four days and achieve 9th place.

The Leaderboard index attracts different kinds of customers. Some prefer to buy the ostensibly better value players who are capable of actually threatening to be (and stay) amongst the leaders, getting on at the very beginning of the tournament at only three or four points with a sizeable stake per point, the aim being to cut and run with a healthy profit as any increase in the spread would yield considerable gains thanks to the relatively high stake. The obvious risk is no different to any other buy, although here, with such a big field for the selected player to contend with, and only eight places on the index, there is a very real possibility that the final make-up will be zero.

Finishing Positions

This is my favourite golf market which, as the name suggests, revolves around the eventual finishing positions in the tournament of individual players. The spread firm will quote a price on each of a selection of golfers, the total usually numbering around 40 or 50 and featuring the better known, leading players and those in form. The only places covered are 1st to 50th, so that for any player who does worse than this is deemed to have a final make-up of 50, whether he actually finishes in 51st place or is disqualified.

The quote for a player reflects the firm's opinion of how the market makers believe that player will perform, the spread typically being three points. The better fancied players might be given an initial price of, for example, 17-20, while most players will be quoted around 33-36.

It is very important to note that the Finishing Positions market does not work in the usual way with buying and selling – here a player is supported with a sell and opposed with a buy, which can be difficult to get to grips with at first, especially if your experience with spreads or indices has been with the stock market.

So, for 'sell' read 'support'. For example, our hero Phil Mickelson might be quoted at 20-23 before play begins in the US Open. If we want him to do well the bet in this case is to sell at 20 because the higher up the tournament he finishes the lower his final position will be. Winning the event means a make-up of 1. On the other hand, predicting and betting on a poor result calls for a buy at 23, and if Lefty then goes on to miss the cut, for example, then the final make-up will be 50, raking in a profit of 27 times the original stake per point (position).

Modern Tour golf is so competitive that nobody has an easy time any more, with the vast majority of a 150-strong field capable of performing well any given week. It is by no means unusual to see top players miss the cut or struggle for the four days to finish well down the field. Consequently, apart from supporting well established, consistent players, in the main it is (in my opinion, at least) going through the list in search of someone to oppose. Of course the potential downside of buying a finishing position at 34, for example, is that we lose 33 times our stake per point if the player wins.

Remember that this market is in-running, being updated after each round. Consequently we are afforded some flexibility as the tournament progresses, with these options to close bets a handy get-out clause whichever of the two positions we have taken. Another good thing about finishing positions is that we know both extremes of the possible make-ups and can decide upon the stake per point accordingly.

No Maximum Finishing Positions

For those who want to oppose a player with a buy of the finishing position but prefer not to have a limited make-up of 50, there is a second market that has no maximum, the higher end of the make-up simply being the field. In return for this luxury of a theoretical extra 100 or so points of profit, buyers must be prepared to pay a little extra, as the spread will be pitched at least several points higher in order for it to be a more realistic reflection of the player's prospects. Conversely, sellers are offered a superior price at the now increased lower end of the spread, but this 'advantage' is relative and only for gamblers with an iron constitution, for the potential losses have now sky-rocketed to become the whole field. Disaster can strike when going low with a no max finishing position – even if your selection has made a dozen consecutive cuts and placed in the top twenty several times in recent outings, selling at a bumper 55 when the sell price at the fixed 1-50 market might be as low as 35 might not look too juicy if the player suddenly plummets down the field, gets disqualified or has to withdraw after eating a dodgy meal. Equally frustrating would be a very poor first round that leaves practically no chance of making the cut followed by an experimental second round, or similar 'practice' play after a poor third round – each wasted shot sends your player further down the field, taking your money with him.

These and other considerations must be taken into account before embarking on a finishing position bet but, with much to help make your mind in terms of information, experience of watching players and an acquaintance with courses and conditions and so on, this market offers considerable opportunity to make money.

Match Bets

Another popular and interesting golfing spread betting opportunity is the two-player *match bet* (again the players' standing in the actual tournament is irrelevant). The long-term, *72-hole match* bet is particularly interesting, the performance of one player relative to his 'opponent' being measured in the number of shots that separate the two at the end of the tournament.

Before the tournament various match-ups between players of similar ranking will be quoted, a typical spread being Player A 'over' Player B at 1-2.5 strokes. In other words 'A' is the favourite of the two, giving 'B' a start of 2.5 strokes. If you believe the superiority will be greater by the end of the tournament you buy at 2.5, while if you disagree with the assessment enough to favour Player B you sell the index at 1, so that should Player B finish three strokes ahead, the profit is 4 units. An unusual feature about this market is that if one player misses the cut and the other makes it, the bet is still on. The two round score of the player missing the cut is doubled to produce a final, four round total (for example, missing the cut with four over par becomes a final score of eight over par), which still has a theoretical chance of being the better of the two if the player making the cut goes on to perform badly over the weekend and post a worse score.

Being in-running, this market has obvious advantages for the well informed.

The *18-hole* match bet is also between two players, but this time over a day's play and with a different scoring system. The winner is awarded 10 points plus 3 points for each shot won by. Thus if the opening quote reads Player A over Player B at 13-16 the favourite ('A') must win by two shots just for buyers to break even. Here a buy of Player A at 16 for a stake of $10 per point would lose $160 if the players concerned finished level. If Player B were to end the tournament five shots clear of his rival the final make-up of the original match-up of Player A/Player B would be negative, at -25, resulting in a loss for buyers of a whopping 41 times the stake. In the event of a player withdrawing or being disqualified during his round, the make-up is deemed to be +25 to the opponent, while a maximum make-up of 55 applies to this market. Considering the possible differences – even over 18 holes – between two players this ceiling makes sense.

Not surprisingly the one-day match bet can be rather volatile. Regardless of even expert opinion as to which player should perform better, on any given day the reverse is quite possible, so you have to be prepared to experience considerable swings of fortune in this particular market. Remember that a number of the better players are slow starters, for example, concentrating on getting the tournament off to a solid, safe start, while less successful players, being used to missing the cut more frequently, can have a more cavalier attitude to the early stage of an event. Such different approaches to tournament play are liable to create ostensibly surprising results over a mere 18 holes. Another factor to take into account here is that there is no facility to get out of the bet once play begins, and the attraction of the spreads is the flexibility that in-running betting provides. Consequently the 72-hole match bet is the less risky, more flexible option, albeit one that leads to lower profits.

Hotshots Index

This is an interesting market based on the performance of nominated golfers. If you fancy several players to perform particularly well (or badly) the Hotshots index lumps a group together with points collectively awarded for their overall performances over the course of the tournament. Usually the format is as follows: 25 points are allocated for each top ten finish (including ties) and there is a 25 point bonus for winning the tournament.

Here is a simple example. Jim Furyk, Davis Love, Tom Lehman and Fred Funk might make up a group called the USA Hotshots, with a quote of 34-38. With this points system only two players need finish in the top ten for the collective Hotshots make-up to be 50 points and a profit of 12 times the initial stake per point. For the make-up to be zero every player would have to finish outside the top ten.

This is one of the many markets that might appeal to sellers, despite the usual risk involved of seeing all the opposed players performing at the top of their game.

US Football

Thanks to 'American' football's increasing popularity outside the USA and expansive live television coverage of the NFL in the UK, for example, throughout the season, the spread firms make sure to feature a host of markets. Among these are the usual 'numbers' spreads such as *Supremacy, Total Points, 1st Quarter Points, Time of 1st Touchdown, Touchdown Scor-*

ers' *Shirt Numbers, Total Touchdown Yardage, Super Bowl 100 Tournament Index* and so on. Below is a selection of other interesting options.

First Last Blast

This market asks you to predict the first and/or last touchdown scorer in a game. The first touchdown scorer is awarded 25 points, as is the last touchdown scorer, while if there is just one touchdown the scorer is awarded 50 points.

Hotshots Index

In this market Sporting nominate four 'Hotshots' from a team. The scoring is very simple – 25 points are awarded for each touchdown scored by any of the nominated players. For example for a New York Giants v Baltimore Ravens match Sporting quoted the Hotshots Index as 40-45, and the players were named as Jamal Lewis, Shannon Sharpe, Amani Toomer and Tiki Barber. The Ravens won but, with Jamal Lewis the only hotshot to score a touchdown, the final make-up was 25 points (25 points per TD). This is an interesting market in that the possible make-ups (other than zero) can to some extent be accounted for because they consist of chunks of 25 points.

Handicap Win Index

This is a handicap (known as the 'line') of a team's dominance over another. A team that beats this handicap when winning the game is awarded 25 points. If they win but do not cover the handicap line the team is awarded 10 points, with zero for losing. Here is how it works:

For a match between the New York Giants and Denver Broncos Sporting made the Giants favourites, giving them a handicap of -7 points. With this in mind their price for them to cover this line (i.e. win by 7 or more points) was 10-13. Therefore if you fancied the Giants to beat the Broncos by more than 7 points you would go high and buy at 13. They won 21-8 and were thus awarded 25 points for covering the line, resulting in a profit of 12 times your stake.

One advantage of the handicap win index over points supremacy is that we know the possible make-ups beforehand. Buying the favourites in this example involves a maximum loss of 13 times our stake even if our selection goes on to lose by 20 points. Had we bought the same team at, say, 7 in a points supremacy spread, then the same 20 point deficit would lose us 27 units (on the other hand, of course, the handicap profits are also clear at start, but finite make-ups are at least in part more manageable).

Player Supremacy

This is an interesting one. For live matches two players are thrown in against each other to see who performs best at their given task. For example two quarterbacks are measured according to the difference in their net passing yardage, while for two running backs the contest revolves around their rushing yardage. It is important to note that a quarterback's passing yards could be negative as any sackings will count as yards lost.

Sporting Index will quote a supremacy price according to who we think is the form player.

For example for a New York Giants versus Baltimore Ravens game, Sporting pitted the two quarterbacks Kerry Collins (Giants) and Trent Dilfer (Ravens) against each other, making Collins the clear favourite by between 35-45 yards. This is another potentially 'negative' market since on any given day either player could significantly out-perform the other, and there is already a sizeable 'start' given to the underdog in the opening quote. In this particular example sellers (at 35) did indeed have their day when Dilfer's net passing yards were 10 more than those of Collins (including yards lost by sackings). With a final make-up of -10, sellers won a handy 45 times their stake, while buyers lost 55 times their stake.

Team Performance

For those with a specific interest in a particular sport the various performance indices are worth a look, and the American football team performance, the aim of which is to predict the quality or otherwise of a team's overall match performance, features numerous components.

Points are awarded for winning, drawing, scoring touchdowns, kicks at goal and sacking the opposing quarterback. However, points are deducted for missed kicks and turnovers. Thus points are awarded/deducted as follows:

Win	25 points
Touchdown	15 points
Field Goal	5 points
Sacking the opposing quarterback	5 points
Missed kick	-5 points
Turnover (not on downs)	-10 points

As an example, for the Tennessee Titans versus Baltimore Ravens match, Sporting quoted the Baltimore performance as 24-28. In fact the Ravens stormed home 24-10 and their performance added up to 80(!), the final make-up being broken down as follows: 25 points for the win, 60 points for 4 Touchdowns (4 x 15) and -5 points for a missed field goal.

By throwing negative points in the mix Sporting have cleverly introduced factors that lend the overall performance a different slant in that there is more to consider than simply scoring points. In this case missed kicks and turnovers can cancel out the team's win, for example.

Soccer

Hailing from England it should come as no surprise that soccer is my favourite sport (I am a life-long fan of Liverpool). Born a year after England's World Cup win I have yet to witness such national glory but, in the meantime, there is a wealth of soccer around the world to watch and to take an interest in. And spread betting really comes into its own with soccer, with countless markets framed around every aspect of the game you can imagine – and then some. I mentioned earlier that fixed odds bookmakers reacted well to the arrival and subsequent emergence of the spread firms, jazzing up their existing markets and creating new ones, offering betting in-running and so on. However, just to put things in perspective in terms of the number of markets spread betting generates, for a *single*, 'live' match during soccer's 2004 European Championships, Sporting priced up an assortment of separate match, team, player and special bets numbering more than 120!

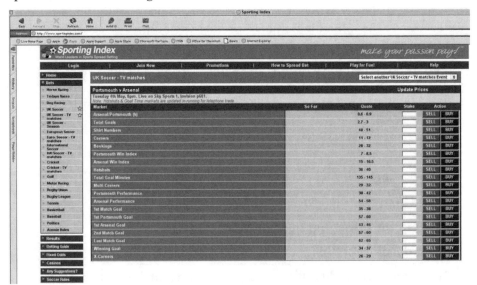

Possible football markets at Sporting Index

Whole volumes could be written just on certain areas of soccer spreads but, as I mentioned earlier, in some ways golf is a better universal example with which to illustrate how spread betting works. Nevertheless, it is interesting to look at the way in which football as a sport is ideal for spread betting.

The usual markets are numerous, and these include *Total Goals, Supremacy* (goals), *Win Index* (25 points awarded to the winning team, 10 points for the draw and zero for a loss), *Goal Scorers' Shirt Numbers, Time of 1st Goal, Total Goal Minutes* and *Individual Player Goal Minutes.*

Here is a selection of others that soccer enthusiasts might find attractive.

Total Bookings

Soccer is a tense sport in which nerves play a large part, and the constant prospect of heavy physical contact combined with match circumstances tends to result in a few players' names being noted down in the referee's book. In fact yellow and red cards are such an important part of the game that the Total Bookings market is a very popular one. Pundits are keen to give their pre-match predictions regarding the extent to which teams or certain players prone to poor discipline will cope and, importantly, what the contribution the referee himself will make in this regard.

The spread firms' scoring system allocates 10 points for a yellow card (maximum one per player) and 25 points for a red card. Note that if a player receives a yellow card and then a second yellow card (i.e. a red card) then he is awarded 35 points (10 + 25).

A typical pre-match quote might be 32-36 points for a 'normal' fixture, which means the firm anticipates between three and four yellow cards. However, the spread will be set much higher for a traditional derby match between, for example, Manchester United and Manchester City or, north of the border in Scotland's Premier League, Glasgow's incredibly tense Rangers versus Celtic clash – each steeped in history and with a large helping of animosity between the two clubs. In these encounters, hyped up to the maximum by the media, the spread can easily open at least a good 20 or so points higher. While this is much higher than the overall average per match (reflected in the first price), with a single 'unpleasant' situation capable of generating several cards, the potential for tempers to flare and the referee to stamp his authority during the 90 minute match is clear to see.

Total Corners

Surprisingly popular, this market is based on the total number of corners accumulated by both sides in a game. For those who 'support' one team in a fixture more than another this has the advantage that you can watch a match without having to worry about who wins.

Goals are what make matches, and the atmosphere created by bookings contributes to the excitement, but corners would appear to lack any such attraction. Moreover, you could be forgiven for believing that, apart from the subject matter being rather boring, an attempt to predict the number of corners in a match is a futile exercise. In fact to some extent the outcome is indeed impossible to evaluate accurately beforehand but, with so much information available on the internet, with statistics specific to particular teams, patterns are there to be seen.

The average number of corners per match is approximately 11, a figure around which the firms will cast their initial quote, the spread itself usually 1 point. Therefore a normal pre-match quote might be 10.5-11.5. This prices then decreases/increases more or less in line with time elapsed/corners won.

For a while I was interested in the corners market, setting up a detailed spreadsheet with a view to selling corners, typically when a run of a number of corners in a short period of time sent the price up, the point being that the game should calm down as other factors come into play. While there is nothing wrong with this strategy from a statistics point of view, there is obviously a considerable element of risk inherent in going short on such a market. It can be stressful and does not suit everyone – indeed it probably didn't suit me as any enjoyment derived from watching the game itself disappears even at the prospect of another corner being won.

Buying can be equally frustrating if, from the moment you get long of the spread – whether this be right at the beginning of the match or a point at which you sense the game has started to open up a little – the corners just don't come. Furthermore, events within the match itself can also drastically alter the course of play and the nature of the struggle. In fact so many factors should be taken into account when contemplating getting involved that the corners market is really a lot more complex as an in-running proposition than most people appreciate – which is why the spread firms are happy to continue to attract the punters.

Nevertheless, an experienced, well informed soccer watcher who is able to spot lulls and other periods of play relevant to the likelihood or otherwise of there being more corners could do worse than to investigate this particular spread.

Multi Corners

This is simply the number of corners in the first half multiplied by the number of corners in the second. Thus four corners in the first half and seven in the second produces a final make-up of 28. However, 10 in the first half and then none whatsoever in the second half makes up to zero (10x0). Remember that, unlike the normal total corners market, this time the actual number of corners won during the match as a whole can be far less significant in determining the final make-up than how the corners were distributed between the two 45-minute playing periods. Another point to consider is that the multi-corners index is updated only at half-time, by which time the damage might already be done. This lack of flexibility compares poorly with the in-running total corners index, which also produces smaller deviations in terms of the final make-up.

By way of an example, the multi-corners quote before a match might be 30-33. If there are five corners in the first half the price will not alter much but, with eight corners, for example, the half-time quote will have risen to around 47-50, despite the fact that there still remains a theoretical chance that – in the event of no corners coming in the second half – the make-up will be zero.

It is also possible to bet just on one team's corners, including multi-corners for each team, while the trivia enthusiast might be interested to know that the usual opening quote for the *Four Corners*, market which is framed around how long it will be until a corner is taken from all four corners of the pitch, is around 60-63 minutes...

Performance Markets

These feature components that – combined – serve to gauge the success of a particular team or player over the course of a match. Not surprisingly goals are included, as are yellow and/or red cards, the two extremes designed to make the punter's decision making a bit more complicated – which is indeed the case – as well as to spice up the betting experience.

Points for Sporting's *Team Performance* are awarded as follows:

Win	25 points
Draw	10 points
Goal	15 points
Clean sheet	10 points
Woodwork (must rebound into play)	10 points
Corner	3 points
Yellow card	-5 points
Red card	-15 points

A 1-1 draw with a couple of yellow cards per team, five corners each and one team managing to hit the woodwork twice in the closing minutes would result in final make-ups of 50 and 30 points respectively. This total is not far off the typical pre-match quotes for evenly matched teams, the spreads possibly being pitched around 34-38 for each.

On the other hand, a comfortable 2-0 victory, with seven corners for the winning team, three for the losers and two yellow cards each leaves us with final make-ups of 76 and -1. This, too, fits in well with a match in which one team is well fancied to win, opening quotes for the favourites being upwards of 60-64, with an apparently cheap 11-14 for their opponents. Notice how easy it is for a team to end the 90 minutes with a negative make-up, and how an accumulation of cards can knock a sizeable hole into an otherwise successful performance.

With eight components in a performance market it is clearly rather complex and should be approached with caution, as is the case with the other firms' offerings. Assuming you join all four firms, then you can look around to see which of these distinctive markets – if any – best suits you. For example IG Index has a quite different concoction, with 25 points per goal, 3 per corner, -10 per yellow card, -25 per red card and a nice twist of 1 point per minute that a team keeps a clean sheet. This time an even fixture might see each team's pre-match quote put at 60-66, with a strong favourite versus minnow encounter throwing out more like 108-115 and 17-23 respectively. Now the result is not enough for us to calculate the make-ups because the actual times of the goals is a major factor.

Note that these markets, while not in-running throughout the match, are updated at half-time, although it is surprising how little can sometimes be gleaned at this point, even after a full forty-five minutes of play and action across the range of performance components. Food for thought.

Similar yet completely independent is Sporting's *Player Performance*, where selected players are awarded various performance points based upon particular events. These are:

Goal scored	25 points
Goal assist	10 points
Shot on target	5 points
Forcing a corner	3 points
Free kick won (including penalties)	3 points
Passing to own player in opposition half	2 points
Free kick conceded	-3 points
Yellow card	-10 points
Red card	-25 points

By narrowing the market down to just a single player (around half a dozen selections are usually available) we are entering specialist territory, and you certainly need considerable experience in watching soccer and specific players before venturing into this bet. So-called playmakers and influential all-rounders such as England's David Beckham and Zinedine Zidane of France tend to be given rather high opening quotes in the 80s and 90s. This is as much based on the greater than average time they are given the ball, allowing them full opportunity to notch up a couple of points with each pass in the opposition's half. Average quotes are closer to 40-45, which seems a cheap buy until you consider that by hardly touching the ball, conceding a few free kicks, picking up a yellow card and then being substituted – in other words by no means an untypical performance even for a good player – all contributes to a negative make-up. Having said that, strikers can hot a rich vein of form and reap rewards for buyers when they figure prominently in one-sided matches but, if you're going to get involved in this market, look to selling the 'star' names at big prices. However good a player is, it still takes a goal, an assist, a fair number of passes and a clean, disciplined game to reach 90+ points, while top players are prone to being substituted once enough damage has been inflicted on the opposition.

Apart from the usual unpredictability the downside here (like the team performance market) is the single update at half-time, but this is another example of how a bit of homework can be a very useful tool indeed, with the each of these components featured in match reports nowadays, thus providing the specialist with enough material to make use of.

Cricket

Just as not all those who like sport like to gamble, not all those who gamble necessarily enjoy watching all sports upon which they wager. Personally, I like watching most sports, but with cricket the attraction is based purely on its potential as an interesting betting medium. In fact this is probably a good thing, as any kind of supporter role or emotional involvement with a game can have negative implications when it comes to taking into consideration certain factors and subsequently making judgements regarding prices and opportunities etc. Of course it is useful to be well acquainted with the ins and outs of a sport on which we risk our hard earned cash, and to those not used to cricket there are rules, terms and aspects of play that can be rather confusing. However, the aim of the game is for one team to make more runs than the other and, with hundreds of runs usually being the norm, hey presto – an excellent and potentially very tasty ready-made platform for betting.

Cricket is absolutely perfect for spread betting. As well as the massive numbers involved in terms of the scores, it is the very peculiarities about the game that invite criticism from its detractors that make for a perfect in-running market as far the sports gambler is concerned. International 'Test' matches, with (in theory) two innings per team, lengthy breaks for meals and what can seem like too leisurely a pace of play mean that these matches are scheduled to take place over five days if necessary.

The longer these events go on, the more markets change, resulting in a host of new prices and new situations that require both the spread firm and the customer to look at the bigger picture.

Here are a few examples of what's on offer.

The Test Match: Total Runs in an Innings

You don't need to be a cricket fanatic to dabble in this market, which simply predicts the total number of runs each side will score in an innings. Of course I would advise against getting heavily involved without closely following the game for a while, but diligent preparation and homework should serve to lay the foundations for sensible betting. As well as watching matches to get a feel of the ebb and flow of different match situations, information is paramount, with enough material out there to get your hands on in terms of the vital statistics that the spread firms themselves use to come up with their quotes.

A typical pre-match quote for England's total innings runs in the first match of a series against Australia, for example, might be 315-325. Now, unlike soccer, where a score as high as 5-0 at decent international level is quite rare, here we are dealing with a make-up that has a potential range of literally hundreds of points.

The experts like to remind us of the importance of all sorts of factors, from how the ball reacts when it comes into contact with the grass, the effects of the weather (rain, humidity), light, dark, how many days/hours of play remain, the teams' respective game-plans and so on. Of course they are correct in going into so much detail but, essentially, a key ingredient of whether a side manages to reach 100 or 600 runs boils down to how well (or poorly) the batsmen bat, the bowlers bowl and the fielders field.

Consequently the constantly updated index – which more or less moves along with each run scored and is adjusted accordingly with each loss of a batsman – effectively ties the spread firm into new positions as a match progresses. With both very high and very low scores quite feasible, the psychology of this market is intriguing, posing a conundrum as to which option is better – buying or selling. Even when all factors have been taken into consideration there will still be arguments for both positions, so it is imperative, as usual, to weigh up the (bad) possibilities.

The very nature of *selling* on such a market, with finite gains and potentially disastrous losses should the team perform exceptionally well, can be difficult to feel comfortable with. I would prefer to sit back and adopt a waiting policy with a view to watching the index rise as the opening batsmen accumulate runs. In believing that a team will struggle to make a decent score we tend to be afraid of missing the boat, prompting us to sell before play begins just in case there is a very quick loss of a batsman and a sudden drop in the spread. This may indeed happen, but such an occurrence does not necessarily put an instant stop to selling opportunities. If it does, then so be it – there is no law that says we *must* bet. Meanwhile, should the match take an unsurprising course, with a steady flow of early runs, the seller is then rewarded for his patience, effectively earning himself bonus points over those who opposed the batting immediately now that the spread has moved up from 315-325 to a juicier 365-375. For *buyers* there is also an awkward decision to make before the players come out – if the star batsmen take the initiative from the very beginning the bargain basement opening price will disappear...

Fortunately for spread bettors the stop/loss facility at least provides some sort of safety net against particularly unpleasant reverses, going some way to taming such a volatile market but not completely breaking the fall.

The Limited Over Match

There is a suggestion here that the risk involved in taking a position in a match with a pre-set limit of 50 overs (300 balls), for example, is minor compared with the numbers experienced with (very) long test matches. This is true, but remember we are still dealing in the main with make-ups that can quite easily hit the 250+ mark. Note also that this time it is the number of overs remaining in an innings – as well as the remaining wickets – that is the key factor in determining the spread.

Individual Batsman's Runs in an Innings

During the course of a match the spread firm will predict the number of runs a batsmen will score in the innings. A typical opening quote might be 30-34, leaving buyers open to a potential loss of 34 units in the event of the player failing to get off the mark. Even at the top level this is by no means rare, although many people are – once again – naturally averse to selling on such a market in case they become locked in to a high scoring performance.

Here we have yet another opportunity to exploit the flexibility afforded us by in-running spreads. Closing out of these total runs markets during play might mean falling foul of the actual spread but, with such big swings of fortune always around the corner, we can be forgiven for putting the breaks on here. Changes in the bowlers, the weather, lapses of concentration and so on mean that each time the batsman faces a new delivery of the ball, hurtling toward him at the speed of a train, the index could be ready for a sharp drop if a wicket falls, while even a brief, two minute period of poor bowling or skilful batting is enough to hike a runs spread up by more than a dozen points. Remember also that even ostensibly modest stakes can lead to considerable losses. Try not to be impatient or greedy and, importantly, don't panic...

In conclusion, the total runs markets are obviously of great interest to the spread bettor and are worth looking into even if you'd never normally think of taking a sporting-only interest in cricket. Furthermore, cricket enthusiasts who have no previous experience of sports gambling should definitely investigate how spread betting, with very flexible in-running markets, presents them with a chance to put their ability to read a game and call on their experience to good use.

Other Markets

Not surprisingly there are various other types of cricket bets for those who consider the game's unpredictability a handicap when it comes to total runs indices. Among these are *Fall of Next Wicket*, which gives you the opportunity to predict when the next wicket will fall. Linked with the total runs markets, this is effectively a bet on the collective performance of the two batsmen currently in play. Whereas the loss of wickets is obviously instrumental in contributing to the eventual overall runs total but not in itself final, here the bet ends as soon as one of the batsmen is out.

The *In-Running Win Index* works the same as in other sports and events, the market awarding 25 points to the winning team, 0 points for a loss or 10 points per team for a draw. However, this is cricket, so the in-running spread tends to move around more than we would expect in other sports, where the nature of a team or player's likelihood of holding on to a lead is usually easier to assess. Ironically, the jokes often levelled at cricket about how the weather is the most important factor are undoubtedly relevant to such markets, where a dominating lead can come to nothing if a match is hit by constant rain. Many a match has been drawn because the team that is a few hundreds runs behind and has no realistic chance of winning manages to hold on by approaching their second innings with nothing other than survival in mind – as opposed to actually scoring any runs. And all the while they will be looking for the heavens to open up, which they are prone to do, this divine intervention losing a lot of money for those who had bought the leading team a day earlier on the win index at, say, 20 points, when victory seemed assured.

The *Tons-Up Index* is a market based on the aggregate of all individual innings scores over 100 (e.g. a score of 155 produces a make-up of 55) for a Test Series (an individual score of 99 does not count). For example at the start of a three Test Series between Sri Lanka and England Sporting Index might predict that the total number of Ton-Ups would be 170, setting the quote at 165-175. Although in theory it is possible that not a single player will manage to reach a century, in practice there may well be a few in-form players who succeed in passing the magical 100 runs mark, and it takes only one outstanding individual innings of 220 to already contribute 120 points to the eventual make-up. Once again the fact that we can trade in-running is incredibly useful.

Horse Racing

There seems to be something magical about horse racing that even manages to tempt those interested in other sports to have the occasional bet. As one of the thirtysomething generation fortunate enough to see spread betting evolve and subsequently become established as a key part of sports gambling, if I were to get involved with horse racing it would be with spreads rather than fixed odds. However, this is by no means an indication that – at least for win purposes, for example – spreads offer superior value, rather it is due to the facility to oppose a horse on the spreads. (Of course this can also be done on a betting exchange – see Chapter Seven).

In fact being able to take a sell position is one of the main attractions of the spreads for horse racing enthusiasts, as the usual advantage these firms offer of in-running betting is clearly impractical in the case of a lightning fast five furlong race, for example, already serving to do away with spread betting's greatest appeal.

Let's take a look at the some of the markets.

Individual Race Index

A bet may be offered about the performance of horses in individual races, awarding points according to official finishing positions. The points structure varies according to how many runners there are in a race. For races with up to 12 runners the points are as follows:

1st	50 points
2nd	25 points
3rd	10 points

Races with over 12 runners taking part are:

1st	50 points
2nd	30 points
3rd	20 points
4th	10 points

Given the available options of either buying or selling a runner in these markets the advantages or otherwise of spreads compared with fixed odds depends very much on whether, as a buyer, we would expect the horse to have excellent winning chances or be a solid 'place' contender. For example a fixed odds win only bet would return a bigger profit if successful than would be the case buying the same selection on the index, but should the selection finish second the fixed odds bet would be a loser while the spread bet would most likely still result in a decent profit.

For help in deciding which format best suits this or that bet it is worth visiting a site such as **oddschecker.com** (see Chapter Five), which has a very useful tool that weighs up the differences in value between a spread bet and the fixed odds each-way bet (the nearest equivalent) by comparing best prices and the returns/losses for each result.

Favourites Index

This market is framed around how the favourites perform in each race at a particular meeting. A winning favourite is awarded 25 points, a second place 10 points and a third place 5 points. In the event of a race starting with joint favourites, the favourite for the purpose of the market is deemed to be the horse with the lower racecard number.

Example

At an Ascot jumps meeting, the Favourites quote might be 56-60 points. If we believe that the favourites will collectively perform better and amass more than 60 points, then we buy at 60, let's say for £10 per point. If at the end of the meeting two of the favourites have won, two have come second and another finished third, then the final make-up will be 75, for a profit of £150. Furthermore, depending on the order of these results, it might have been possible to close out for a bigger profit.

Stop at a Winner

Another favourite index, here the focus is on how many races on a card will elapse before a favourite wins. The make-up is 10 times the number of that race. In the event of there being no winning favourite, the make-up will be ten times one more than the number of races on the card, i.e. 80 points on a seven race card with no winning favourite. Note that a favourite which dead heats for first place is treated as an outright winner.

Example

Back at Ascot, the opening Stop at a Winner price might be 28-31, a rather low price for this market that suggests the presence of well fancied favourites in the first two races. If indeed the favourite in the first race does deliver, then the make-up is 10 points – bad news for buyers who opposed the favourites.

Match Bets

What will be the distance – in lengths – between two nominated horses at the finish? This conundrum, as in golf, for example, throws two competitors into their own private race. The maximum distances for the purpose of these bets is 12 lengths in a Flat race and 15 lengths in a National Hunt race. In this market whole points are divided into tenths, so buying for £10 per point translates to £1 per tenth.

Remember that this market is concerned only with the performances of the two horses relative to each other, irrespective of where they finish in the race proper.

There are other markets, such as *Winning Distances*, the *Jockey Index* (along the lines of the Favourites Index) and one based on the starting prices of the winners. Generally, because the in-running facility is not present with horse racing, I would suggest viewing the race index as another string to the sports bettor's bow in that it offers more flexibility depending on the aim of the selection. As for the other markets, however, these tend to be exclusive to spread betting and therefore might be of specific interest to those who know their way around a race course.

Tennis

Not surprisingly Wimbledon accounts for the lion's share of the year's betting but, with more tennis and sport in general being shown on television, other tournaments are also becoming reasonably popular, with familiar, standard totals and supremacy markets being the usual on offer. Here is a selection.

Match Supremacy

This is effectively a match bet that awards the victor 10 points for winning the match and an additional 5 points per set won by. The maximum make-up is 25 points, with the minimum being -25 (for three set matches these are 20 and -20 respectively). With such a scoring system this – not unlike golf's 18-hole match bet – leaves the punter open to considerable losses if the result goes the 'wrong' way.

Game Supremacy

One would expect a market framed around the total of games won by Player A versus total games won by Player B to be simple but, alas, this is not the case. Despite the conclusive, finite results producing a winner and a loser, here we have a perfectly feasible, albeit ironic possibility in that the eventual winner of the match will not necessarily be the winner of the game supremacy match, as winning more sets doesn't automatically mean winning more games. For example the story of the match might read 7-6, 4-6, 7-6, 1-6, 6-4 in which case the winner's tally amounted to 25 games while the loser notched up 28. Factor into the equation the fact that players are prone to conserving energy once they fall too far behind in a set, deciding that to invest too much effort would be futile and counter-productive, and the prospect of a player effectively letting a set go at, for example, 0-3 down and 0-40 in the fourth, and a reasonably logical strategy by our selected favourite can have serious implications regarding the bet. This is a very important issue when weighing up the pros and cons of this market. You've been warned.

Total Match Games

This is simply a bet on which we take a position on how long a match will be in terms of the number of games played. Typically the earlier the match is played in a tournament the lower the quote, while as a tournament progresses, and the higher seeds begin to play amongst themselves, the firms will pitch their quotes a little higher to reflect the higher potential of a close match. Sellers should not forget that even the final set of a hard-fought match can hike up the final tally, and buyers can come unstuck when (as I mentioned above) a player abandons a set instead of putting up stiff resistance.

As usual with in-running markets there is more to making a profit than simply taking a position on either side of the spread and then waiting for the match to end – this would be no different to an old fixed odds bet. The best way to increase your chances of success is to closely watch the game for an indication of how it might pan out – the in-running aspect of spread betting is there to be taken advantage of.

Tournament Total Games

An interesting long-term market for the bigger events that centres on the total number of games played in every match! Not surprisingly the numbers can be rather intimidating but that is not to say the market is to be automatically avoided unless you have an enormous bankroll. These are often the very markets that are worth investigating because the in-running facility affords us considerable flexibility and time for the price to eventually settle down if the opening matches go against our initial position, while it is possible that an early run of results creates an opportunity to close out with profit. In the days leading up to Wimbledon 2004 Sporting's quote was 4700-4750, with a built-in allocation of 38 games for each incomplete match or retirement.

X-Courts

A variation on soccer's multi-corners market, this deals with the aggregate set 'multi-games' for a match. For example the multi-games total of a single set in which the score is 6-2 is 12 (6x2). Therefore a long match with a score line of 6-4, 6-7, 6-1, 2-6, 6-3 leads to a total X-Courts make-up of 102 (24 + 42 + 6 + 12 + 18). Not surprisingly this can be a volatile market, which explains why there is a maximum make-up of 400! Buyers should keep in mind that a five set thriller does not necessarily lead to a massive make-up, while a set won to love counts as zero in the calculations...

Motor Racing

Motor racing does not perhaps attract the same level of betting as the more popular sports but it still creates considerable interest.

Drivers Points Match Bet

A similar match bet to those seen in golf, this puts two drivers against each other, irrespective of the part they play in the race as a whole. The driver who finishes ahead of the other will be awarded 10 points plus 2 points per position he wins by. Note that in the case of a driver retiring it is the point in the race at which he comes off that determines his actual finishing position. For example if a driver is the third man to spin off/crash/retire in a 20 man race, he has finished 17th.

The advantage of these match bets is in not having to weigh up a driver's overall prospects, instead being able to concentrate on his chances against just one other competitor. For example in the Monte Carlo Grand Prix, Sporting might make Michael Schumacher favourite over brother Ralf with a spread of 2-5 points. If big brother Michael just scraped on to the podium after finishing 3rd with Ralf further down the field in 10th, the make-up of the market would be 24, this being 10 points for finishing higher, plus 7x2 points for being 7 places above Ralf in the final standings, resulting in a profit of 19 units for those buying the several times world champion at 5 points.

However, had Michael been the fourth driver to retire with 22 drivers having started the race, he would have been judged to have come 18th, so with Ralf again finishing 10th the make-up of Michael (the favourite) 'over' Ralf would then be -26 (10 points for winning plus 16 for the margin of victory, expressed as negative because the underdog won). Having given Ralf 5 points even before the race began, buyers would lose a total of 31 times their initial stake. Given that retirements and accidents are part and parcel of motor racing, it stands to reason that such a match bet in this particular sport presents a potentially more hazardous range of outcomes than is normally the case (and even in more 'predictable' sports the risk element is already considerable).

Non-Sporting Events

If we are what we eat then, from a gambling perspective, we are what we watch. That television companies put so much effort into outbidding each other for the right to broadcast sport is great for bookmakers, but in recent years television has also presented firms with other, non-sporting events around which a market can be based. This is particularly true of the more flexible spread firms, for whom anything that involves numbers and variation is a market in the making. Step forward the so-called 'reality' show.

Ironically, television series featuring 'real' people, the typical man or woman in the street laying themselves open to the scrutiny of the eager viewing public, have become so successful that each new wave of 'contestants' seems increasingly aware of what is required to exploit whatever publicity they generate (often irrespective of their actual success in the show itself). Learning with them has been the gambling world, which has managed to get wise to how shows such as Big Brother can be used to both generate income and attract new custom.

As with some of the novelty markets mentioned earlier, these non-sporting events make for interesting betting opportunities. The Outright Win index for *Big Brother*, for example, which awards points to the first six places in the 12-participant competition (60-40-30-20-10-5) often undergoes extreme changes during the first two or three weeks. Unlike golf, soccer or US football, for instance, where the spreads makers formulate markets based on their expertise in the field, experience and hard facts, with a television show involving unknowns the market makers have no better idea than we do as to how long this or that competitor will survive. Consequently the nature of each participant's market price is such that a favourite with an early spread of 32-35 can suddenly drop down to single figures. Conversely, it is not unusual for those down in the bargain basement end of the win index at 4-6 to emerge from initial tensions or other events within the *Big Brother* compound to head the market after more than quadrupling in price. The spread firms don't like unpredictability, and this is a major factor in this kind of show.

Pop Idol is another good betting medium, accounting for 1% of Sporting's bets in 2003. Put in the context of a total of 2.7 million bets, and we're talking serious gambling here. Again, like *Big Brother*, competitions like *Pop Idol* give the punter considerable scope to gauge the state of play in-running. The spreads framed around the percentage of the total votes garnered by each of the new set of potential evictees generate considerable interest among viewers with hitherto little or no experience of spreads. Of course the fixed odds firms also get involved in terms of winners markets and evictions and so on but the spreads provide constantly updated in-running markets.

The latest addition to the voyeur market is the popular *I'm a Celebrity...Get Me Out of Here* shows, while Sporting has widened its number of markets to include the likes of the *Eurovision Song Contest*, whose 2003 edition attracted over 2000 bets. We can also bet on the film world's 'Oscars' awards which, ironically, accounted for one of Sporting's unfortunate reverses, the firm suffering a hefty loss on the movie *Titanic* when their prediction of how many Oscars it would win fell short of the final tally.

To sum up, while most of us prefer to stick to the more familiar grounds of sports gambling, spread betting does in fact offer the dedicated couch potato and would-be behaviour expert the opportunity to exploit what are essentially ostensibly unpredictable but nevertheless readable long-term preferences of the television public. I'm sure there are very serious gamblers out there who relish the prospect of getting involved with the *Big Brother* index and who, year after year, make good money.

Money for Nothing

Occasionally an opportunity might present itself that allows us to both buy and sell a selection in the same market to guarantee a profit at absolutely no risk. Such a situation is known as *Arbitrage* and is obviously worth looking out for. Let's say, for example that Sporting have golfer Chad Cambpell's finishing position in the US Open at 33-36, while IG Index put him at 28-31. By simply selling with Sporting at 33 and buying with IG at 31 we have made a profit of two units regardless of whether he wins the tournament or fails to make the cut.

While we would expect the firms to guard against putting themselves in a position where their price is out of sync with the others, with Sporting, for example, sometimes producing 1000 markets in just a week it is possible that a few such situations might arise.

The secret for the punter is to get in quickly before the markets are 'corrected' and everyone is once again singing from the same hymn sheet. The danger, of course, is executing the buy half of the bet, for example, and then seeing the sell price alter enough to render the *arb* redundant, leaving us with either a genuine bet in a market we know little or nothing about or having to close out the bet for safety's sake and perhaps making a loss in the process.

What I would certainly not do is give money to a service that specialises in finding arbitrage opportunities and delivering them to its clients for a fee. The best arb is one you find for yourself, whereas a service could well be providing the very same arb information (something which clearly has to involve a potentially significant delay) to a hundred other hopefuls who will subsequently be trying to pounce at the same time. Furthermore, in order to make these opportunities pay it is necessary to have considerable funds at our disposal. For instance with our golf finishing position example, above, for a locked in profit of just £20 we would have to wager £10 per unit, buying at 31 and selling 33. Although it doesn't matter where Campbell finishes, if he wins the tournament we would win £320 for the sell bet but lose £300 for the buy half. And the longer the event, the longer our money is tied up.

Another problem with arbitraging is that two firms might have different rules for the same sport so that certain incidents during the event might result in different make-ups. Clearly there are risks involved in the (rather greedy) quest for free money – and so there should be. The choice is yours.

Spread Betting Psychology

Perhaps even more than is the case with fixed odds betting markets, spread betting prices are heavily influenced by the public and the media and so on. Moreover, the very nature of spread betting – with the movement of an index very much driven by shifts in direction and demand – opens the way for the more astute sports bettor to exploit his fellow punters' behaviour.

There is a great deal to consider when delving into the psychology of spread betting, but it is enough to mention here people's perception on buying and selling a spread, the two options being poles apart. In general the safest of the two choices is considered the *buy* because the maximum downside is already a known fact. For example buying on the Total Goals market for a soccer match at 2.9 involves a limited maximum liability of 2.9 times the stake per point. Selling at 2.6, on the other hand, leaves the bettor open to much greater losses which, even if a stop/loss is in place, could theoretically cause some damage to the bank roll. As well as the lower downside, most gamblers are also attracted to buying because they are tempted by the potentially high gains, whereas selling looks almost boring in terms of profit because these maximum returns are already known.

However, it is unusual for a soccer match to have so many goals. When this does happen the sellers get their fingers burned and the buyers have cause to celebrate but, during the course of a season, sellers will fare better than the buyers. This is because the fact that the vast majority of punters prefer to buy rather than sell is built into the price, as is the case with most markets in which the sell option involves the greater exposure and the lesser rewards.

While I am not advocating you exclusively sell, it pays to monitor a market from the perspective of the betting public, the point being to recognise when public buying demand has led to top heavy prices in order to buck the trend and grab the value presented by the sell level. Remember too that by being able to bet in-running adds further flexibility to such an approach because popular misconceptions that surround all sports often lead to inflated prices. For example a specific incident during play might be given too much significance by the viewing public, whose erroneous read on the incident manifests itself in a sudden urge to get long on markets they think might be affected, resulting in turn in juicy sell prices.

If a bank roll can cushion the blow of a string of sell bets that meet with high make-ups, then it is worth investing time in learning more about the seller's approach.

Good luck.

Financial Spread Betting

Since spread betting has its roots in the mechanics of financial markets it should come as no surprise that sports gamblers who prefer spread betting to fixed odds can also test their skills with financial spread betting. Instead of a golfer's tournament finishing position or the number of goals in a soccer match, spread bettors today have branched out into predicting, for example, the closing (daily) level of the Dow Jones Industrial Index or other markets.

A leader in financial spread betting is the aptly named *Finspreads* (**www.finspreads.com**), which was launched in April 1999 and, in early 2004, boasted over 16,000 clients worldwide. Based in the City of London and regulated by the Financial Services Authority, the company offers clients the opportunity to buy or sell the world's individual shares, stock markets, currencies, metals and commodities in the same way we have seen in our sporting examples.

Fully embracing the potential of online betting in February 2001 alongside the emerging sports spread betting firms, Finspreads now takes well over one million trades a year, further enhancing its interactive online trading platform in November 2003.

Testing out the Financial Waters

Finspreads also offers new customers a free, eight-week Trading Academy course designed to introduce and subsequently guide clients through each aspect of financial spread betting, a field that can indeed seem rather intimidating to those of us more used to monitoring the progress of Tiger Woods or the unpredictability of US Football's fiery touchdown scorers' shirt numbers market (which is, incidentally, a complex proposition, I can tell you).

Additionally, Finspreads holds free trading seminars for both the beginner and the more experienced trader, designed to help clients determine what type of trader they are and to help in recognising and understanding other important factors and issues such as optimum trading strategies.

As a taster, here is a screenshot, from the Finspreads website, of a so-called streaming quote, which would follow the selection of a particular market.

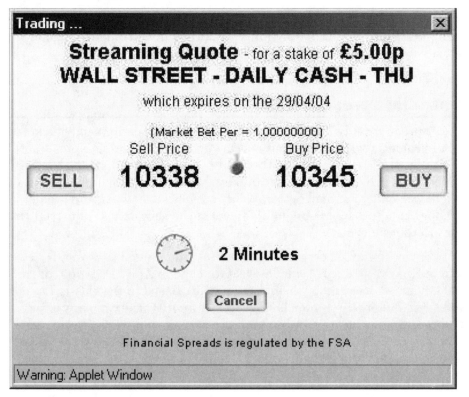

As is the case with sports spread betting we can either buy or sell on the index in order to take a position on the future state of the market. These markets have a habit of showing sharp and sizeable changes quite unlike those experienced in the more finite parameters of certain popular sports markets. Consequently (obviously) it is necessary to become acquainted with the world of finance, but this is not a problem nowadays. Just as there is a great deal of information on the internet with which sports gamblers can keep up to date and which helps in the decision making process, so there is no shortage of sites that can well equip those willing to make the effort in financial spread betting.

With this in mind, perhaps the most useful facility afforded Finspreads' new customers is that, during the eight weeks of the Academy, online clients can trade for as little as a penny per point. I'm not sure whether this option was on offer a few years ago when I first ventured into financial spread betting, but my ego and/or impatience anyway led to considerable swings of fortune in my endeavours to branch out from my usual domain of sports betting into the financial sector. Needless to say such a transition is at best 'interesting' and at worst expensively foolhardy, and I would have benefited greatly from being able to adopt an approach using enough real money to prompt serious effort without assuming the risk of coming seriously unstuck.

The world of online financial spread betting is certainly worth investigating if the concept of spread betting generally suits you. Fortunately it is now possible to take realistic, tentative steps in that direction for minimal outlay.

Chapter Seven

The Betting Exchange

A New Enemy

The emergence of spread betting drastically altered the dimensions of the playing field where sports gambling was concerned by introducing a new betting format and thus giving the punter an alternative approach to gambling. That was a big change indeed but, when betting exchanges came along, the shift was so devastating that a brand new playing field was created. The new millennium might have caused a media frenzy but sports bettors were much more impressed by the significance of the other new arrival that accompanied it.

The age old gambling war between them and us – the bookmakers and the punters – in which the mighty bookmakers had been able to effectively create their own self-serving environment and consequently win battle after battle had come to an end. Betting exchanges offered a quite different scenario that allowed punters to square up against a new enemy – themselves. And this time the competition, while becoming incredibly fierce, nonetheless had a more gentlemanly flavour, with each market tending to offer the bettor more favourable odds than the traditional bookmakers, whose collective monopoly was suddenly under threat from the very sports gamblers whose supply of opportunity they had succeeded in controlling for generations.

Cutting out the Middle Man

Betting exchanges were able to take the gambling world by the scruff of the neck by marrying two key factors – the insatiable appetite of a gambling public eager to flex its betting muscles, and the ability of the internet to bring these punters together in a cyberspace meeting place. The internet has – obviously – paved the way for all kinds of innovative ventures and services over the years but, as far as sports betting is concerned, its role as a medium through which ordinary punters are able to do business with each other – leaving the bookmaker out in the cold – couldn't be more appropriate.

In this chapter we will concentrate on how the idea works in practice, using the Big Daddy of betting exchanges – Betfair – as a model. There are numerous other sites that provide the very same service of so-called matched betting, two major players being Betdaq and Sporting Options. Depending on how much betting exchanges will feature in your sports gambling, you might want to check out some of the growing number of sites now in business with a view to joining a few of them. While essentially singing from the same hymn book, each tends to have its own identity, and the more you have access to as a client, the more opportunities present themselves.

Betfair is the brainchild of Andrew Black, a former professional punter and derivatives pricing modeller who founded the company alongside present Director Edward Wray, a former Vice-President at JP Morgan debt capital markets, in June 2000.

Bringing together counterparties with directly opposing views has resulted in odds that have been estimated at as much as 20% better than the starting prices offered by the conventional, margin oriented bookmaker. This alone is enough to generate interest among the traditional sports bettor, but the fundamental, pure nature of person-to-person betting and the facility to lay outcomes (act as bookmaker) have been responsible for the betting exchange revolution.

Here are a few Betfair facts and figures that should help illustrate just how far, and in such a short time, betting exchanges have come.

- In its first month Betfair matched less than £50,000 of bets per week, yet within a year that weekly figure had risen to over £1 million. It is now in excess of £50 million.

- Betfair turns over approximately £2bn a year.

- Betfair has 200,000 registered customers in 85 countries.

- Over 500,000 bets are matched every day – at a peak rate of 12,000 a minute.

There are other, similarly impressive milestones but you get the picture, and the health of the betting exchange industry is such that other firms are able to compete and co-exist with the market giant, while the exchange phenomenon itself has seen further developments in 2004 (see below). One more thing – predictably, given the general poker boom, in the first half of 2004 Betfair made a deal with CryptoLogic to develop an online poker site.

Unfortunately, detractors and traditional bookmakers continue to point out what they believe to be wrong with the current state of play regarding exchanges, the greatest criticism concerning suspicious betting patterns and the facility to back a losing outcome. Whatever problems that might exist are thought to be in the horse racing industry, but it is of course possible to manipulate outcomes in other sports, too. Given that we didn't live in an ideal world before betting exchanges arrived it might seem unfair to single them out as a breeding ground for cheating, but the debate is sure to continue, perhaps justifiably if it dissuades those who might seek to exploit the relatively new format.

In the meantime the exchanges obviously want their customers to feel confident when contemplating wagers and, with this in mind, Betfair made a ground-breaking agreement in June 2003 with the Jockey Club, signing a Memorandum of Understanding (MoU), effectively agreeing to waive customer confidentiality when betting patterns merit serious investigation. This was followed by further MoU agreements with the Association of Tennis Professionals, the International Cricket Council, the Football Association and even the Darts Regulation Authority.

Serious Fun?

With gambling in general under the microscope as different governments endeavour to work out how its ever-increasing popularity might best be monitored and – in some cases – developed with regulation in mind, in the UK, for example, the band of expert punters who patronise betting exchanges are in danger of coming under fire. Would it be appropriate and fair for sports gamblers who succeed in making a living from laying bets on betting exchanges to be required to register with the Gambling Commission? To label these experts as so-called 'non-recreational layers' simply because they win money from losing recreational players seems ironic but, with the old firm bookmakers having to share bits of their gambling cake with individual betting exchange layers while simultaneously paying all the costs inherent in running such a big business, a call for change is understandable.

As far as the sports bettor is concerned, it would be foolish not to see what betting exchanges have to offer, whether possible advantages are better prices for the backer or opportunities for the layer. In fact if you can't recognise how a betting exchange could enhance your gambling experience, then you've been doing something wrong.

Let's have a look at what's on offer.

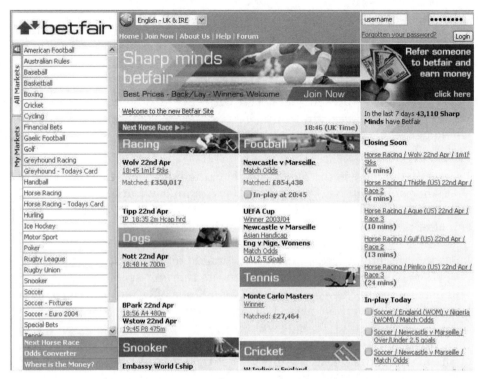

Betfair Homepage

How Does it Work?

Quite simply, sports gamblers log on to a betting exchange such as **www.betfair.com** which provides information about the odds across a vast range of events that other punters are prepared to take a position on. People with opposing views on the same event can make a wager between themselves. Incidentally, we don't know against whom we are betting because our privacy and bet confidentiality is maintained by Betfair's secure site. Of course because bets are matched between people with opposing views the concept is practicable only as long as there are sufficient clients to generate sufficient interest, but with the phenomenon quickly attracting wide scale popularity among sports gamblers it is now possible to find someone with whom to bet even in the case of ostensibly obscure events.

By now you will have noticed the magical ingredient betting exchanges afford the punter that he has hitherto been denied – namely the facility to oppose an outcome, essentially adopting the role of the bookmaker. This is the key attraction to many of today's sports gamblers who have flocked to the exchanges, and the reason why traditional bookmakers – with their considerable operating costs – can't have been too pleased when Joe Public was given the opportunity to effectively set up his cyber stall and steal away their business by taking bets from their longstanding customers.

Playing at Laying

Betting exchanges present the bettor with several advantages over conventional bookmakers, but being able to oppose a competitor opens up a whole new way of sports betting and represents the area in which a new breed of betting animal now roams.

Laying an outcome is the opposite of backing it – we are instead betting that something will NOT happen. If, for example, we are sufficiently confident that in a US football match Team A will not beat Team B, then we can offer all-comers a price of 3.0 (traditional odds: 2-1), let's say with a maximum liability of £200, and wait for someone to take up the challenge. Meanwhile, those Team A fans unable to find such generous odds elsewhere can log onto Betfair, click on the relevant sections of the sports and betting menus, see our ostensibly generous offer and match the bet by placing £100 on their team, at which point we have assumed the role of bookmaker. Should Team A win and our judgement prove wrong, then they win their bet and we make a loss of £200. However, if Team B wins, or the match is drawn, we simply pocket the stake of £100 (minus a small commission – see below). In other words, of the three possible outcomes of the match, by laying a team we were able to bet on two of them.

It is true that before betting exchanges it would also have been possible to oppose Team A in this example by placing separate wagers on both Team B to win and the draw, but this double bet would offer less value than laying the single outcome. Moreover, with some sports it would be practically impossible to oppose a competitor or outcome (for example with an exchange we can lay a golfer in a 150 player tournament).

Fear of the Unknown

After years – generations – of backing it might prove awkward to suddenly try to put ourselves in the bookmaker's shoes when considering the possible outcomes of this or that sporting event. We do tend to dismiss the prospects of a horse or a golfer, for example, when weighing up a betting market, but usually this is done only as part of an elimination process, sorting out the main contenders from the decent chances, maybes, doubtfuls and absolute no-hopers. Now the more adventurous sports bettor can switch sides and abandon the cause of the backer in favour of forming part of a growing opposition, using the same judgements that used to be almost an inconvenience when trying to establish who or what had winning chances to instead determine which participants are worth opposing.

Once we are capable of thinking along these lines the next step is to grow accustomed to the fact that – in most cases – laying an outcome involves being prepared to offer someone odds that leave the layer open to greater liabilities than would need to be wagered by backing an outcome to return the same profit. Perhaps this is an even bigger psychological obstacle than getting used to the laying facility itself. As with any kind of gambling, approach laying with a degree of caution because it would be easy to assume that we can simply build up a fortune by taking bets from suckers looking for a big win at odds of 50-1, for example. Even a successful long term strategy runs the risk of wiping out a bank roll before there is a chance to get going if initial results go the wrong way and the outsiders come in.

Laying Golden Eggs

For the alert betting exchange user these sites can be very profitable hunting grounds, and it is not unusual to guarantee a profit by taking a position, keeping an eye on price changes and then 'closing out' with a bet that ensures a profit regardless of the outcome of the event – just as is the case with spread betting. Exchange betting specialists will get a feel for which sports and events might see considerable market movement, seeking to exploit certain situations by laying a hot favourite at, say 1.83 (or 5-6 in fractional odds) because they expect that competitor for one reason or another to eventually lose support and consequently drift in the market, at which point they then back the same selection at a considerably higher price and probably won't even bother checking the result, which is now irrelevant as far the wager is concerned. Conversely, a selection might be backed at 11.0 with the expectation that later support will see the price fall to a point at which laying it will lead to a sure profit.

Marrying the facility to both back and lay the same selection for guaranteed profit is obviously going to attract the would-be crafty gambler looking for easy pickings, but these opportunities don't fall in the user's lap, while concentrating on predicting specific market movements requires considerable appreciation of the subject matter, patience and nerve. Blindly backing and laying to later close out can be a risky business, a common downside being locked into bets you would have otherwise neither made nor accepted should the magical price change not come.

Choosing Your Odds

Odds quoted on Betfair are decimal odds (see Chapter Five), referred to on the site as Digital odds. The advantage of digital over traditional, fractional odds is that they allow more price intervals and therefore make for tighter prices, greater competition and in turn more opportunities to trade bets.

While backers can shop around the bookmakers to find the best price, we are nevertheless at the mercy of their odds makers. Although a wide scale lack of action on what might be considered poor odds can occasionally lead to the firms having to bow down to punter power and lower their margins, these alterations tend to be minor and we are still obliged to take often unattractive odds in order to get involved.

On exchanges such as Betfair, however, there is always a choice of what odds to accept. Much of the time users are happy with available odds and there should be enough volume of betting to ensure that bets are *matched* immediately,

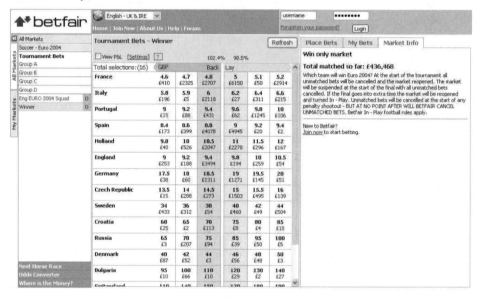

Typical Odds Market

Note that the amount of money available to be matched is given with each price.

Placing an Order

If the odds currently available are not to our liking, then we can simply place an *order* for a better price – obviously this order has to be within realistic boundaries because for the system to work there has to be someone willing to lay the bet at those odds. Conversely, someone looking to oppose an outcome will get no takers if the odds he offers are too skinny. What tends to happen is that as the beginning of an event approaches the market begins to hot up a little, with the odds available undergoing considerable changes as the volume of bets increases.

As well as not being satisfied with the odds on offer, another reason to place an order is when we want to place a bet for a larger amount than is currently available. This situation arises, for example, when we want to back Tiger Woods in a 72 hole match bet with Ernie Els, are happy with the odds on offer, intend to wager $500 but the layers are willing to (collectively) risk only $300. In this case we will be 'filled' in the $300 available, while the remaining $200 will be left as an order. This facility to anyway place an *unmatched* bet as an order guarantees a smooth operation of the system, particularly in view of the fact that this is an automatic process in the case of unmatched parts of bets.

It is always possible to cancel any order that has not yet been matched but, once a bet has been matched, it cannot be cancelled. (If a bet has already been part-matched then you can only *cancel* the outstanding amount.)

Note that even if a bet shows up as being available when you begin to place your bet, it could be cancelled or taken by another customer before you have the chance to match it. The status of all open bets can be checked at any time by going to *My Account* and clicking on *Current Bets*, the same report being automatically when logging on and off.

Bet Execution

Because betting exchanges have software that compares the existing lay prices with those available to back and then automatically matches the orders, by placing an order for a particular bet level on to the system's database we can also take advantage of the software's ability to find us the best possible price – even if this is ultimately more favourable than the one we specified in our original order. For example, if we are happy to back Brazil 2.5 for £150, and the available odds are 2.5 for £150 and 2.6 for £100, then when we place the order at 2.5 for £150 the system will automatically give us the £100 at 2.6 and slot in the remaining £50 at 2.5 as an unmatched bet.

Additionally, after leaving an order on the system at 2.5 for a modest £10, soon after which someone else leaves an order at 2.5 but this time for £1000, the first come, first served rule means that we will always get filled first, regardless of our much smaller stake.

It is quite possible, then, to see a single bet split up according to what is and isn't available at the time. Therefore the intended bet on Brazil at 2.5 for £150 might break down as a matched bet for £100 at 2.6 (best execution), a further £20 at 2.5 with the remainder not filled. This will appear as 3 separate lines on the matched and unmatched bet history report, with all having the same Bet ID so that the original bet can be identified.

Getting Paid

Betfair's system guarantees that the winner gets paid. As soon as a bet is matched the funds to cover the maximum liability are taken from both counterparties' accounts and held in a separate bank account. When the outcome is known, the winning party receives the dividend, less a commission of between 2% and 5%.

Commission

The customer does not pay tax at Betfair, and commission is only paid on net winnings on each market. This feature is particularly beneficial if we have multiple bets on a single market because, irrespective of how many win, commission is calculated only on NET winnings. Note that if bets in a particular market amount to a net loss there is no commission to pay.

With Betfair there is a special incentive based scheme which structures the user's commission rate according to how much action he sees, employing a sliding scale between 2% and 5%. Each Betfair user is allocated a level on a weekly basis (but actually calculated on spending over a much longer period), more bets leading to less commission. It is worth noting that although Betfair has around 200,000 live registered customers, most of its commission comes from its top 1,500 punters, who each make upwards of £15,000 each year.

Betting Opportunities

There are various methods by which punters can back their judgment using betting exchanges. Here are a few of them.

Betting In-Play

'In-Play' betting – what the spread firms call betting in-running – is an important facility that allows users to continue to back and lay outcomes after an event has begun. When a market is In-Play the betting process operates in almost the same way as usual, a crucial difference being that when we place our bet, whether this is to match another bet or to place an order, there is a deliberate time delay before the bet is processed (indicated by the In-Play icon on the betting slip).

The time delay exists to allow those people who have orders on the system to cancel and change their bets if something dramatic happens during the event. A typical example of such a situation occurs in soccer when a team scores a goal – in this case someone who has left an order to back the other team might want to immediately cancel their bet and change to a new level.

Additionally, in order to give users further protection, when a market goes In-Play all existing orders will be cancelled first and the market immediately reopened. This enables us to leave an order on the system a while before the event in the knowledge that (if it has not already been matched) it will be cancelled automatically before the event begins.

Thus far we have been dealing with the simple 'win, lose or draw' type odds markets that are just the same as what we have been used to with bookmakers, only carried out on a betting exchange amongst ourselves. However, fully exploiting the flexibility of decimal/digital odds, betting exchanges also provide their customers with the option to challenge each other with other, trendy, betting formats.

Line Betting

Line betting is essentially an even money bet (i.e. the odds are 2.0) in which we take a position on either side of the *Line* at a particular price. This Price could represent anything from the total number of runs in a cricket match, goals, points and so on to the winning score of a Major golf tournament, the line referring to a line of numbers representing all possible results. In order to bet you either Buy or Sell the Line at the particular price, depending on whether you believe the final result will be above or below this price. The final result will always be an integer. Therefore *Selling the Line* means to placing an even-money bet that the final result will be less than the price at which we sell. For example, returning to cricket as a great sport for betting, let's say that we want to bet on an individual batsman's total runs and thus sell the line at 60.5 (predicting that the player will reach 60 or less runs). If our stake is £50 we will receive £100 (including the stake) if he falls short and lose £50 (the stake) if he makes 61 runs or more. Conversely to support the player we would buy the line at 60.5.

Note that when the difference between the price at which we buy and the final result is less than 0.5 the return from our bet will be less than even-money. In other words the net profit or loss will be less than the stake. For example if we buy the batsman's runs at 47.8 for £100 and he scores 48, then our net profit is £40. (If he had scored 49 or above we would have doubled our money, while a score of 47 or below would lose the £100 stake).

We can be forgiven for finding this a little confusing, so a bit of explanation wouldn't go amiss. In order to fully understand how this latest example works we should treat a bet that is priced between an integer and half-value as two separate bets, split proportionally between the prices. Thus a bet for £100 at 47.75 is effectively the same as a bet for £50 at 47.5 and another for £50 at 48, so that if the result is 48 the first bet wins and the second bet stands, resulting in a net profit of £50. With this in mind, a bet for £100 at 47.9 is equivalent to a bet for £20 at 47.5 and another for £80 at 48 etc. The following table illustrates the profit/loss for various scenarios:

Net Profit/Loss Bet £100 stake	Final Result (Total Runs 47 or below	48	49 or above
Buy @ 47.5	£100 loss	£100 profit	£100 profit
Buy @ 47.75	£100 loss	£50 profit	£100 profit
Buy @ 47.8	£100 loss	£40 profit	£100 profit
Buy @ 47.9	£100 loss	£20 profit	£100 profit
Buy @ 48	£100 loss	Even	£100 profit
Buy @ 48.1	£100 loss	£20 loss	£100 profit
Buy @ 48.2	£100 loss	£40 loss	£100 profit
Buy @ 48.25	£100 loss	£50 loss	£100 profit
Buy @ 48.5	£100 loss	£100 loss	£100 profit

Range Betting

This is Betfair's facility to engage in person to person spread betting, something that – as you will see later in this chapter, has become another area of interest for the operators now that matched betting is obviously here to stay. A format with which we should by now be familiar, in range betting we buy or sell at a particular price, the unit representing a run, goal, minute and so on, depending on the event. The stake is always quoted per unit. We SELL when we expect the result (final make-up) will be less than the market price and BUY when we believe it will make up more. A popular range bet would be framed around the total goals in a soccer match, for example.

Minimum & Maximum Limits

While spread betting firms often introduce limits in order to avoid extreme swings and potentially awkward liabilities, betting exchanges also have their own reasons to impose a minimum and maximum limit on the price allowed on any range bet (such limits can occur naturally, of course, depending on the sport/market etc.). Remember that in the case of Betfair, for example, the site itself is not taking any bets, with practically all the money wagered passing to and fro between the users themselves. Consequently it is in everyone's interest to limit the maximum potential loss on every bet placed, in doing so guaranteeing that each customer has sufficient funds in their account to cover their total exposure so that every winning bet can be honoured.

Index Bets

Also a form of spread betting, Index bets allow users to back and lay on markets framed around awarding points for performance and eventual outcomes in an event such as a 50-25-10 win index for a Grand Prix race. These markets might be of special interest to spread bettors looking for additional opportunities.

New/Old Kids on the Block

Having seen the extent to which betting exchanges have eaten into the monopoly of fixed odds betting once enjoyed by traditional bookmakers, it probably won't come as a surprise that the concept of matched betting itself has resulted in the creation of variations on the theme, with new firms emerging that provide the online gambler with even more flexibility. While these latest operators have something different to offer users, the common denominator is that each site is devoted exclusively to person-to-person betting.

Binexx.com

Launched in March 2004, **Binexx.com** specialises in providing a binary betting exchange that features financial, sports, political and other markets. Once you have got used to the likes of 'standard' exchanges such as Betfair the chances are you'll be tempted to give the binary version a try.

Binary betting involves betting on the percentage chance that a specified event will occur. If the event does occur the binexx market is settled at 100, while if it does not the market is settled at 0. Therefore we BUY if we expect the event to occur and SELL if we don't. The site has the usual features such as in-running betting and placing orders, although the commission set-up is different. Rather than profit, here the charge is based on 50% of the risk per point.

How it Works

All bets have a maximum potential loss. For example if we place an order to buy an outcome at 51, for every pound we want to buy we will need £51 in the account – in other words £2 per point at 51 would need £102 in the account (plus commission).

However, selling at 49 also requires the same funds as we are open to a potential loss of 51 times the stake per point. The rest is easy.

Binary Price/Fixed Odds Conversions

The following table shows prices converted from traditional fixed odds into the binary equivalent.

Sell	Fixed Odds	Buy
99.0	99/1	1.0
98.8	80/1	1.2
98.7	75/1	1.3
98.5	66/1	1.5
98.0	50/1	2.0
97.1	33/1	2.9
96.2	25/1	3.8
95.2	20/1	4.8
94.1	16/1	5.9
92.3	12/1	7.7
90.9	10/1	9.1
90.0	9/1	10.0
88.9	8/1	11.1
87.5	7/1	12.5
85.7	6/1	14.3
84.6	11/2	15.4
83.3	5/1	16.7
81.8	9/2	18.2
80.0	4/1	20.0
77.8	7/2	22.2
75.0	3/1	25.0
71.4	5/2	28.6
66.7	2/1	33.3
60.0	6/4	40.0
55.6	5/4	44.4
50.0	evens	50.0
44.4	4/5	55.6
40.0	4/6	60.0

We can see that a buy and sell of 50 is an evens bet (obviously), while a buy of 20 means that we are backing an outcome that is a 4-1 chance (20% probability) and so on.

Cantor Spreadfair

Cantor Spreadfair, only a few weeks in existence at the time of writing (June 2004), is the world's first spread betting exchange. It is a sign of the times that the domain of betting exchanges is considered to be such a growth area that one of the latest operators looking for a new angle is already a major player in online betting, Cantor Index being one of the four spread betting firms. Combining arguably the two most innovative developments in betting, namely spread betting and the person-to-person exchange (and all made possible thanks to the internet, of course), does indeed seem like an effective means of attracting the modern online sports bettor.

By allowing its clients to bet directly against each other Spreadfair affords them the flexibility to choose their own prices rather than those offered by spread firms (including Cantor itself...). Consequently, when users are able to buy or sell the soccer corners market, for instance, at the same level, then both sides have saved money compared with betting with the spread firms by virtue of the fact that on the exchange there is no spread.

The usual facilities are there such as placing an order to receive the best price, while commission is based upon net winnings in any market, set at an opening level of 5% and featuring an incentive scheme based upon betting volumes.

When it was first launched **cantorspreadfair.com** concentrated on the European Soccer Championships, but by the time you're reading this expect to find the site has a range of sports and events as full as other exchanges.

I must say that I had been expecting a spreads exchange to appear eventually, and I am not sure what the implications will be for the established spread betting operators. What is clear is that they will have to offer better prices or at least shorten their spreads once their clients take a serious interest in the exchange format.

Chapter Eight

The Future

Everyone dreams of seeing into the future, and gamblers in particular would find such a gift rather useful. It would be great to know where online gambling will be a few years from now and, although we'll have to wait and see, I would be surprised if the more mainstream nature of both gambling in general and internet gambling does not result in the whole industry enjoying a healthy existence well before 2010.

Before turning to a few final thoughts, here's a taste of what the future might hold in terms of both potentially good and bad.

Real Virtuality

The UK horse racing industry has had its fair share of scandal during the last year or so but, despite the threat of punters turning to other sports for their betting release, has managed to survive pretty well. However, an area of fun or novelty gambling has now been introduced into a traditional bookmaker's markets and, regardless of its frivolity, is probably at least a minor irritation for the horse racing industry.

The cheeky new kid on the block is none other than scheduled Virtual Horse Racing. In itself virtual horse racing software is not new, and while surfing the internet checking out gambling and gaming sites we are sure to stumble upon virtual racing somewhere along the line. It is even possible to place wagers of sorts on some sites. But this latest development takes the phenomenon a very important step further.

In 2004 Bookmaker William Hill became the first firm to add virtual racing to sports book stable as part of the site's overall betting market! Now its customers can take up a unique opportunity to include a bet on Tiger Woods to win the US Open, the Chicago Bulls to lift the SuperBowl, Smarty to beat all-comers and Jim Dandy, the No.10 at the 7.50 race at the completely fictional Greenside Park all in the same multiple bet.

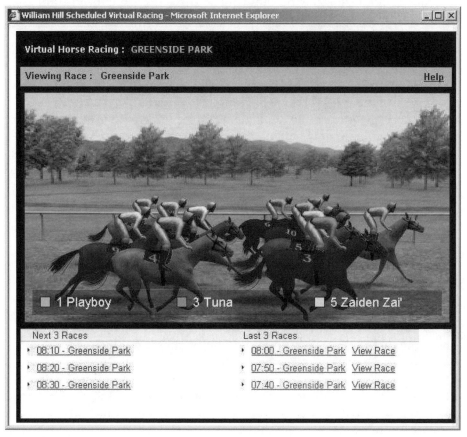

And they're virtually off!

Whether enough people will be happy to team up their selections in major sporting events with a computer graphic remains to be seen, but bookmakers tend to know what they're doing and have a habit of successfully anticipating the trends of the gambling public. People are into all kinds of gambling on the internet, and Greenside Park plays virtual host to non-stop action throughout the day, every day of the week, with races every 10 minutes. From an entertainment point of view the races could last a bit longer, but others will probably be introduced as interest takes hold. In the meantime the graphics are okay and it is even possible to watch re-runs and consult a results section(!), but the key is gambling. There are bets from as little as a penny, while it is possible to win up to £50,000 per day!

The Twilight Zone

For those gamblers happy to sit in front of their computers wagering their real money on pretend horses every ten minutes, developments in interactive television means that (in the U.K.) they will also be able to have similar flutters by switching over the channel on the TV when the end credits of the late night film begin to roll. Virtual horse racing, accompanied by greyhounds, might even be joined by rodents! The Television Gaming Group, behind Avago and iSportsTV interactive channels on Sky, are planning the launch of live gerbil racing. It might seem that we are entering the twilight zone of gambling here, but these latest developments in the quest to present the betting public with 'fun bets' is simply an indication of how betting has evolved (purists out there might well question this choice of word). In the good old days the betting world was complex and reasonably varied but nevertheless finite in terms of supply and demand, with commonly accepted boundaries in which both the bookmakers and the bettors did their business. Today, on the other hand, racing organisations are justifiably concerned about the prospect of seeing their role in the betting industry being undermined by computer-generated horses.

Meanwhile, fun betting promises to create a whole new breed of bettors who, the marketing people clearly hope, will then join the ranks of the more traditional punters. When I told my father – a skilled numbers man who knows a great deal about gambling – of the fun aspect of virtual horse racing, he likened it to the lottery, saying it was just 'gambling' (you can see Dunnington senior is big on philosophy). Of course he is making a perfectly valid point, but from a man whose definition of a 'fun' bet is one that brings a smile to the face when the winnings are counted, the potential attraction of 'novelty' betting is non-existent. But different strokes for different folks, as they say, and whoever came up with the idea of gerbil racing as a means to generate interest and business was not thinking about my dad. Here's something for you to ponder – my family moved from suburban England to a quiet village in Scotland in late 2003. The village has a population of about 400 and is surrounded by rolling hills and countryside with forests and lakes and chocolate box views. The village hall is used for all sorts of local events, and my two-year-old daughter goes to a cosy weekly playgroup there. In a fortnight the hall will host – and not for the first time – an evening of .... yes, virtual horse racing. This is the face of the brave, new and unashamedly virtual world of gambling.

And what about this... We had some family come visit recently and the subject of conversation soon latched on to a form of 'cartoon' racing I'd found during my countless hours trawling through the internet – namely 'bottom' racing (and all for your benefit, I might add). It had another name that shouldn't really be repeated on these pages, and although you could make only a pretend bet the idea of watching six bottoms (no legs – or any other body part come to that – just bottoms) racing to the finish line was judged to be worthy of the real experience to these members of my family. Of course (apart from sending some rather worrying signals about my family) it is obvious where my dad stands (or, indeed, sits) on the viability of cartoon bottom racing as a betting medium, but – and those marketing people take note – if such a facility were to be introduced, with races every few minutes, I can guarantee that people would be happy to risk their money on the outcome. Whether there would be any interest at my village hall I don't know, but on the internet – a bet is a bet.

Anyway, back to the present, bottomless virtual gambling world, and the combination of betting and the attraction of interactive television are set to explode if recent research is anything to go by. Market analysts Screen Digest, for example, forecast that interactive television betting will turnover (□4bn) US$4.87 billion by 2007, with gross margins of (□709m) US$864.7 million. The U.K, thanks to regulatory reform, looks to account for up to two thirds of this, with bingo and casino-style games expected to be a major pull. The second largest single market is expected to be France, and lotteries could be raising as much as €1bn by 2007.

And this brings me to a prediction – as soon as it becomes legal (and it will), the U.K. will see interactive, web-based gambling games in pubs, clubs and specialised 'fun' gambling establishments, just as the leisure industry currently caters for thousands of networked bingo players around the country every night of the week. Where drinkers can now see live sport there will be big screen gambling.

Keep it virtual.

Web Attacks

Even the occasional internet user is well aware of the potentially destructive virus, but internet gambling sites are specifically susceptible to the so-called 'Denial of Service' (DoS) attack which typically results in an annoying, albeit temporary, inability to act within the site.

Unlike the virus, which tends to be fairly indiscriminate in terms of where it strikes, such an attack is designed by the perpetrator with specific targets in mind, the aim being to hold an internet gambling site, for example, to a form of cyber ransom (although DoS attacks are security breaches they tend not to be designed with security or confidential information in mind).

Often the victim will be a company/user that finds itself deprived of certain services and, consequently, unable to function properly, a common and particularly inconvenient experience for website customers being the loss of network connection and, consequently, operation. This can be achieved by the attacker by flooding servers with information requests, fake data packets used as ammunition with which to threaten firms into paying up or being shut down. Most of these organised gangs operate from Eastern Europe or Latin America, while some use a network of infected 'zombie' computers in other countries.

Imagine, for example, thousands of online poker players who have been playing in a big tournament for a few hours being suddenly unable to participate, unsure as to what the problem is exactly, unable to log back on and, ultimately, making a mental note to try another site next time. Similarly, sports gamblers already committed to an in-running bet who are unable to access a site quickly enough to make further moves or modifications are also seriously affected.

Indeed the attackers are at their most threatening in the run-up to a major sporting event. The prospect of many, many thousands of sports gamblers and enthusiasts getting ready to place their bets with a well-known online bookmaker as one of the year's most important events is about to get underway, only to 'lose' connection is a nightmare for these firms. Put in this context of mutual frustration we can see just how effective such attacks can be, and how damaging even a temporary period in which a company is forced out of operation. Even if we sympathise with the online firm and understand the kind of problem they are experiencing, we are nevertheless sufficiently frustrated to look upon that particular site rather negatively – an emotion that is exactly what the perpetrators are out to achieve.

Attacks can also harm or destroy a computer system's programming and files and so on, but it is the threat/execution of maximum inconvenience that is usually the underlying theme, the point being simply to deprive the target of two essentials – time and money – with a view to pressuring the firm into acquiescing to what has become an internet extortion racket.

Earlier this year British police worked with online bookmakers in an effort to combat this modern form of blackmail through the threat of DoS attacks in the weeks before one of the horse racing world's elite events, the Grand National, which also happened to take place within 48 hours of a crunch FA (soccer) Cup semi-final clash between Arsenal and Manchester United, two of the world's biggest clubs. With bookmakers expecting around £50m (US$92.8 million) to be wagered such attacks could prove problematic in the extreme. Indeed one UK based online betting exchange was reportedly subject to such an attack, the website being deliberately hit with so much data that it was disabled for almost two days, thus affecting more than 15,000 customers. A demand for 40,000 Euros to avoid further disruption was ignored, the matter was left in the hands of Britain's National Hi-Tech Crime Unit, subscribers were assured that their personal details had remained safe and the site was soon up and running. Other top online bookies also fell foul of DoS attacks which, although they appear to be manageable, are nonetheless to be expected in the future when we gamble online.

Prediction – The problem with DoS attacks will get worse rather than better, and operators will need to make concerted efforts to address the issue as the perpetrators find new and improved methods of causing wide scale disruption. That is not to say casinos and bookmakers will suffer more severely from the attacks than is the case today, rather that it will be imperative to have some sort of co-operation between prospective targets, Internet Service Providers and web security experts in order to be more collectively prepared.

Final Thoughts...

...and predictions.

Prediction

Rather than bitter competition I expect to see B&M and internet gambling to share more common ground. To some extent this is already happening, with major 'live' poker tournaments seeing their ranks swell with internet qualifiers and B&M casinos' poker rooms expand thanks to the internet revolution. Meanwhile the novelty of sitting at home in front of the computer while watching your bets being played out on a roulette wheel in a B&M casino on the other side of the world has a good chance of blossoming into a viable industry niche.

Prediction

Online casinos that provide only one part of the overall internet gambling experience will suffer if they fail to branch out into other areas. Again there are signs of the necessity to expand in that a number of operators have already embraced other formats, most notably casinos and bookmakers keeping up with the game by opening their own internet poker rooms. Ideally, a site will offer its customers a casino, poker room and sports book.

Prediction

If enthusiasm for European soccer gambling is anything to go by, Asia will emerge as a major player in terms of the numbers involved in internet gambling.

Prediction

Regulatory bodies, industry leaders, customer-friendly organisations, jurisdiction and licensing representatives and governments will work towards the creation of international, industry standard regulations. I admit this is wishful thinking on my part, but perhaps (for example) the UK's fairly sensible, practical approach to regulation will prove inspirational to other governments in finding some sort of productive, common ground.

Prediction

There will be an explosion of casino based mobile phone gambling.

Prediction

Poker will continue to evolve and grow beyond all predictions.

Prediction

Someone reading these pages will win $1 million online...

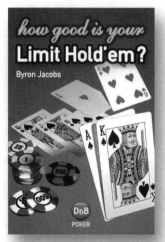
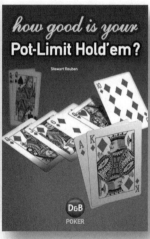